THE ULTIMATE ZERO POINT WEIGHT LOSS SOLUTION

Achieve Your Wellness Goals with an Empowering Approach that Combines Flavorful, and Over 1700 Days of Easy-to-Make Recipes

Ivy Villasenor

© Copyright 2024 by Ivy Villasenor - All rights reserved.

The content of this book is provided with the intent to offer accurate and reliable information. However, by purchasing this book, you acknowledge that neither the publisher nor the author claim expertise in the topics discussed, and any advice or recommendations are provided solely for entertainment purposes. It is recommended that you consult with professionals as necessary before taking any action based on the content of this book.

This disclaimer is recognized as fair and valid by both the American Bar Association and the Committee of Publishers Association, and is legally binding across the United States.

Unauthorized transmission, duplication, or reproduction of any part of this work, whether electronic or printed, including the creation of secondary or tertiary copies, or recorded versions, is prohibited without the express written consent of the publisher. All rights not expressly granted are reserved.

The information presented in this book is deemed to be truthful and accurate. However, any negligence in the use or misuse of this information by the reader is their sole responsibility, and under no circumstances will the publisher or the author be liable for any consequences or damages that may arise from the use of this information.

Furthermore, the information contained in this book is intended solely for informational purposes and should be treated as such. No guarantees are made regarding the ongoing validity or quality of the information. Trademarks mentioned are used without permission and their inclusion does not constitute an endorsement by the trademark holder.

TABLE OF CONTENTS

CHAPTER 1: UNDERSTANDING THE ZERO POINT SYSTEM 9
1.1 The Philosophy Behind Zero Points 10
1.2 How the Zero Point System Works 11
1.3 Benefits of Zero Point Weight Loss 12

CHAPTER 2: BUILDING A HEALTHY RELATIONSHIP WITH FOOD 15
2.1 Mindful Eating Practices 16
2.2 Overcoming Emotional Eating 17
2.3 Setting Realistic and Sustainable Goals 18

CHAPTER 3: NAVIGATING COMMON DIETARY CHALLENGES 21
3.1 Balancing Zero Point Foods with Other Nutrients 22
3.2 Managing Portion Sizes and Serving Suggestions 23
3.3 Eating Out and Social Events: Staying on Track 24

CHAPTER 4: PRACTICAL MEAL PLANNING STRATEGIES 27
4.1 Efficient Grocery Shopping Tips 28
4.2 Meal Prep Techniques for Busy Lifestyles 29
4.3 Creating Balanced and Satisfying Meals 30

CHAPTER 5: INTEGRATING HEALTHY HABITS INTO YOUR DAILY ROUTINE 33
5.1 Incorporating Physical Activity 34
5.2 Stress Management and Self-Care Practices 35
5.3 Tracking Progress and Staying Motivated 37

CHAPTER 6: DELICIOUS ZERO POINT BREAKFAST RECIPES 39
6.1 Energizing Morning Smoothies 39
- Green Detox Smoothie with Spinach and Apple 39
- Berry Blast Smoothie with Almond Milk 40
- Tropical Mango and Pineapple Smoothie 40
- Creamy Avocado and Kale Smoothie 40
- Sunrise Citrus Zinger 41
- Green Ginger Peach Delight 41
- Berry Beet Bliss 42
- Cucumber Mint Refresher 42
- Sunrise Citrus Zinger Smoothie 42
- Green Tea Mint Medley Smoothie 43

6.2 Hearty and Healthy Breakfast Bowls 43
- Quinoa and Berry Breakfast Bowl 43
- Chia Seed Pudding with Fresh Berries 44
- Zesty Tofu and Spinach Scramble Bowl 44
- Smoked Salmon and Avocado Bowl 45
- Sunny Mediterranean Breakfast Bowl 45

Berry Almond Breakfast Quinoa 46
Greek Yogurt and Fruit Parfait Bowl 46
Oatmeal with Cinnamon and Sliced Apples 46
Sunrise Salmon and Avocado Bowl 47
Mushroom and Spinach Frittata Cups 47

6.3 Quick and Easy Breakfast Options 48

Overnight Oats with Almond Butter and Banana 48
Veggie-Packed Egg Muffins 48
Whole Grain Toast with Avocado and Tomato 49
Cottage Cheese with Pineapple Chunks 49
Zesty Ginger-Peach Yogurt Parfait 50
Savory Spinach and Mushroom Egg White Cups 50
Warm Cinnamon Apple Quinoa Bowl 51
Spicy Tomato and White Bean Toast 51
Sunrise Smoothie Bowl 51
Peppered Mushroom & Spinach Omelet 52

CHAPTER 7: SATISFYING ZERO POINT LUNCH RECIPES 53

7.1 Fresh and Flavorful Salads 53

Grilled Peach and Chicken Salad 53
Zesty Lime Shrimp and Avocado Salad 54
Crispy Tofu and Kale Salad with Tahini Dressing 54
Beetroot and Goat Cheese Salad with Walnuts 55
Tangy Citrus Fennel Salad 55
Asian Slaw with Peanut Dressing 56
Mediterranean Chickpea Salad 56
Spicy Watermelon and Cucumber Gazpacho 57
Roasted Beet and Goat Cheese Salad 57
Asian Sesame Edamame Salad 58

7.2 Wholesome Sandwiches and Wraps 58

Turkey and Avocado Lettuce Wrap 58
Grilled Chicken and Veggie Wrap with Hummus 59
Tuna Salad Lettuce Wrap with Pickles 59
Egg Salad Sandwich with Whole Grain Bread 59
Zesty Lemon-Pepper Tofu Wrap 60
Smoked Salmon and Cucumber Nori Rolls 60
Spicy Chickpea and Spinach Wrap 61
Grilled Vegetable and Goat Cheese Burrito 61
Chimichurri Chickpea Salad Wrap 62
Spicy Grilled Veggie & Hummus Wrap 62

7.3 Warm and Comforting Soups 63

Chicken and Vegetable Soup 63
Butternut Squash and Carrot Soup 63
Tomato Basil Soup with Grilled Shrimp 64
Lentil and Spinach Soup 64
Saffron Infused Cauliflower Soup 65
Miso Mushroom Broth 65
Lemon Pepper Veggie Soup 65

Spicy Tomato and Red Lentil Soup 66
Miso Umami Soup 66
Creamy Roasted Cauliflower Soup 67

CHAPTER 8: NOURISHING ZERO POINT DINNER RECIPES 69

8.1 Protein-Packed Main Dishes 69

Zesty Lemon Dill Baked Salmon 69
Grilled Chicken Breast with Asparagus 70
Colorful Shrimp Stir-Fry with Broccoli and Peppers 70
Herbed Turkey Meatballs with Marinara Sauce 71
Zesty Lime & Herb Turkey Quinoa Bowl 71
Savory Spinach & Mushroom Stuffed Bell Peppers 72
Herb-Infused Chicken and Root Vegetable Roast 72
Garlic Lemon Baked Tilapia 73
Zesty Lemon Basil Tilapia 73
Spiced Chickpea Stuffed Bell Peppers 73

8.2 Vegetable-Centric Entrees 74

Stuffed Bell Peppers with Quinoa and Vegetables 74
Roasted Cauliflower Steaks with Chimichurri Sauce 75
Spaghetti Squash with Tomato Basil Sauce 75
Grilled Portobello Mushrooms with Balsamic Glaze 76
Spiced Cauliflower and Chickpea Stew 76
Sesame Ginger Tofu Stir-Fry 77
Baked Spinach and Artichoke Hearts 77
Roasted Eggplant with Tomato Relish 77
Savory Spinach and Artichoke Galettes 78
Curried Cauliflower with Lentils 79

8.3 One-Pot and Sheet Pan Dinners 79

One-Pot Chicken and Quinoa with Spinach 79
Sheet Pan Baked Cod with Vegetables 80
One-Pot Turkey Chili with Beans 80
Roasted Salmon and Fennel with Citrus Herb Sauce 81
Spicy Paprika and Garlic Shrimp 81
Lemon Thyme Chicken 82
Mediterranean Vegetable and Chickpea Stew 82
Lemongrass Infused Tilapia Bake 83
Smoky Paprika Chicken Skillet 83
Herbed Lemon Shrimp and Asparagus 83

CHAPTER 9: GUILT-FREE ZERO POINT SNACKS AND DESSERTS 85

9.1 Savory Snacks to Curb Cravings 85

Spiced Turmeric Roasted Chickpeas 85
Cool Cucumber Yogurt Bites 86
Savory Egg & Sea Salt Snackers 86
Parmesan Zucchini Chips 87
Zesty Lime Shrimp Ceviche 87
Smoked Salmon and Cucumber Rolls 87
Herbed Tofu and Veggie Skewers 88

Beetroot and Feta Cheese Dip 88
Zesty Lime Shrimp Skewers 89
Rosemary-Infused Mushroom Caps 89

9.2 Sweet Treats Without the Guilt 90

Baked Apples with Cinnamon 90
Mixed Berry Sorbet 90
Frozen Banana Bites with Dark Chocolate Drizzle 91
Chilled Grapes with Lime Zest 91
Chia and Coconut Yogurt Parfait 91
Spiced Pumpkin Mousse Cups 92
Pear and Ricotta Spice Boats 92
Zesty Lemon FroYo Bites 93
Chai Spiced Poached Pears 93
Zesty Lime Yogurt Freeze 94

9.3 Healthy Party Platters and Appetizers 94

Grilled Zucchini Roll-Ups with Herbed Goat Cheese and Peppers 94
Spiced Cauliflower Bites with Cilantro Yogurt Dip 95
Cherry Tomato and Mozzarella Pesto Skewers 95
Smoked Salmon Cucumber Cups 96
Mini Mediterranean Frittata Muffins 96
Roasted Red Pepper and Artichoke Tapenade 97
Chilled Ginger Peach Soup 97
Zesty Lime Grilled Shrimp Skewers 98
Creamy Baba Ganoush with Pomegranate 98
Savory Mushroom Mini Tarts 98

CHAPTER 10: FOUR-WEEK MEAL PLAN 101

10.1 Week 1: Jumpstart Your Journey 102
10.2 Week 2: Building Momentum 102
10.3 Week 3: Maintaining Balance 103
10.4 Week 4: Sustaining Success 103

CHAPTER 11: TIPS AND TRICKS FOR LONG-TERM SUCCESS 104

11.1 Adapting the Plan to Your Lifestyle 104
11.2 Staying Inspired and Informed 106
11.3 Celebrating Your Achievements and Setting New Goals 107

THANK YOU FOR YOUR PURCHASE! 109

CHAPTER 1: UNDERSTANDING THE ZERO POINT SYSTEM

Imagine you're at the grocery store, scanning shelves packed with tantalizing options, each label screaming for your attention. Now, picture yourself navigating this maze easily, confidently selecting foods that not only taste delicious but also propel you toward your wellness goals, all without the hassle of tallying calories or tracking every bite. This harmonious balance between simplicity and nutrition is the core of the Zero Point System, a revolutionary approach designed to help you eat well, lose weight, and feel invigorated without feeling trapped by endless diet rules.

The beauty of the Zero Point System lies in its simplicity. It categorizes foods based not just on their calorie content, but on their overall nutritional value and their ability to satiate. Foods that score zero points are those that are nutrient-dense yet lower in calories—foods you can enjoy freely, without the guilt or the math. These are the ingredients that form the backbone of your meals, ensuring that you're nourished, satisfied, and energized.

But how does this translate into real life, especially when you're juggling work deadlines and family commitments? Through the upcoming pages, we'll explore not only the science behind the system but also how it seamlessly integrates into your hectic everyday life. You'll learn how these zero point foods can be transformed into quick, mouth-watering meals that enthrall the senses while keeping your wellness goals on track.

As we embark on this journey together, remember that understanding the Zero Point System isn't just about learning which foods to choose. It's about reshaping your relationship with food. It's about moving away from a punitive calorie-counting exercise and towards a more joyful, intuitive way of eating. Let's step into this promising path, one flavorful, zero-point meal at a time, crafting a lifestyle that's as fulfilling as it is delicious.

1.1 THE PHILOSOPHY BEHIND ZERO POINTS

Diving deep into the philosophy behind the Zero Point system is like embarking on a voyage to uncharted territories with a map that guides you to a treasure of wellness and vitality. At its core, the system is pledged to transform the weary battles against weight fluctuations into a triumph of good health and intuitive eating. It fundamentally shifts the conventional paradigm of dieting from restriction and deprivation to abundance and nourishment.

Let us start by unravelling the conventional wisdom surrounding dietary regimes. Traditionally, diets have been about numbers — counting calories, tracking carbohydrates, or measuring portions. While structured, these methods often strip away the joy of eating and can lead to cycles of quick fixes rather than sustainable health. Enter the Zero Point System, which turns the focus from merely subtracting harmful elements to emphasizing the addition of wholesome, nutrient-rich foods. These are foods that not only encourage weight loss but also foster overall health, making them free to be enjoyed without tallying points or enduring guilt.

At its essence, the Zero Point philosophy believes in the power of food as medicine — not just a fuel but a remedy that heals and strengthens the body from within. Foods given a zero-point value are selected based on their high nutrient density and low energy density. These include a variety of fruits, vegetables, lean proteins, and whole grains. The common strand among them being their ability to satisfy hunger efficiently while providing ample vitamins, minerals, and other essential nutrients without excess calories.

This innovative approach also centers around satiety and satisfaction. It's no secret that feeling hungry can sometimes lead to poor food choices. By prioritizing foods that are filling and gratifying, the Zero Point system naturally regulates appetite and curbs cravings, making weight loss a more pleasant experience.

The philosophy stretches beyond what we eat to also encompass how we eat. Zero Point encourages mindful eating — a practice where you tune in to your body's signals of hunger and fullness and make conscious food choices in response. This means eating when you're physically hungry and stopping when you're comfortably full. Mindful eating respects the body's intrinsic wisdom and fosters a healthier relationship with food.

Moreover, embracing this system can be a cornerstone for long-term health gains. For instance, frequent consumption of high-fiber zero point foods like fruits and leafy greens can enhance heart health, improve digestive functioning, and even lower the risk of certain cancers. The dietary approach also tends to be low in sugar and unhealthy fats, which aligns perfectly with guidelines recommended for preventing chronic diseases. Beyond individual health benefits, the Zero Point philosophy promotes a way of eating that is sustainable for life. Unlike restrictive diets that often lead to a yo-yo effect — where you lose weight only to regain it — zero point foods can be enjoyed in abundance, ensuring that you feel continuously supported without feeling deprived. This aspect addresses one of the critical challenges in weight management: keeping the weight off permanently.

In aligning with modern lifestyles, the ease of integrating zero point foods into daily routines cannot be understated. For busy parents or professionals, being able to prepare simple, wholesome meals without extensive preparation or ingredient tracking can free up time and mental space. This ease significantly enhances the likelihood of maintaining these healthy eating habits long-term.

Furthermore, the Zero Point plan is not just about individual health but also considers family and community wellness. It encourages preparing meals that the whole family can enjoy, fostering healthier eating habits among children and creating supportive environments for sustainable health. This communal aspect of eating can strengthen bonds among family members and friends, reinforcing the social dimension of eating well.

The Zero Point philosophy also holds a mirror up to current food culture, asking us to reevaluate our relationship with food and diets. It challenges the notions of fad diets and quick fixes, advocating instead for a more holistic, balanced approach to eating. This system helps rekindle the joy of eating for health, pleasure, and energy simultaneously—without the burden of complex rules or the shadow of potential failure.

In summary, the philosophy behind the Zero Point system is based on a powerful assertion: food is not just a collection of calories and nutrients to be rigorously managed, but a source of pleasure, health, and life. It integrates scientific principles with empathy towards human nature, recognizing that the path to sustainable health is not made through restrictions but through a welcoming abundance of the right choices. A truly revolutionary approach is transforming how we think about dieting, bringing a promise not only of weight loss but of lasting wellness and joy in eating. This approach is not just a diet but a new way to live—a paradigm shift towards enduring health and vitality, celebrating food as a precious ally in our journey towards a fulfilled and energetic life.

1.2 How the Zero Point System Works

Navigating the principles of the Zero Point System might feel akin to learning a new language. At first, the concepts seem foreign, perhaps a bit complex, but as you immerse yourself, it becomes second nature— a path that feels both intuitive and rewarding. Now, let's unfold how the Zero Point System intricately works, weaving the fabric of a diet plan that not only simplifies the journey of weight loss but also turns it into a harmonious lifestyle.

The cornerstone of the Zero Point System is its categorized list of foods that are deemed "zero points." These are foods you are encouraged to consume without the need to meticulously count each calorie or track every portion. Wonderfully, these foods are recognized for their high nutrient density—think colorful fruits, vibrant vegetables, whole grains, and lean proteins. The strategy behind this categorization is rooted in the understanding of energy density and nutritional quality, focusing on foods that provide maximum nutrition for minimal calories, ideally ones that can help satiate hunger efficiently.

Let's illuminate this with an example. Imagine a plate filled with grilled chicken, broccoli, and a small portion of whole-grain rice. The chicken and vegetables here represent zero-point foods, emphasizing that you can eat generous portions of these without tipping the scales on calorie count. The idea is that these foods fill you up, not out— they satiate you deeply, reducing the temptation to reach for less wholesome, high-calorie options.

The mechanism of how this works within your body is fascinating. When you consume zero point foods, you're not just avoiding empty calories; you're nurturing your body with fibrous, voluminous, and protein-rich foods that stabilize blood sugar levels and decrease hunger pangs. This is pivotal, as fluctuating blood sugar levels can often lead to cravings, impulsive eating, and eventually, weight gain.

Transitioning through a typical day under the Zero Point approach, breakfast might include a hearty portion of oats (a zero point food) topped with fresh berries and a dollop of non-fat Greek yogurt. For lunch, a vibrant salad with assorted veggies, sprinkled with seeds, and dressed in a light vinaigrette serves not just satiety but also packs in nutrients without piling calories. Dinner could be stir-fried veggies with strips of flank steak, allowing a fulfilling meal with the flexibility of zero point foods.

Importantly, the system isn't meant to restrict but rather to guide your eating habits towards more nutritional wealth. There's practical reasoning embedded in choosing which foods are determined as zero points. These decisions are backed by a wealth of scientific research indicating their benefits in promoting satiety, reducing overall calorie intake, and maintaining muscle mass, which is critical in the metabolism-boosting process.

Moreover, the Zero Point System is ingeniously designed not to be static but dynamically adaptive to individual needs. It understands that each person's body, lifestyle, and preferences differ. Thus, while the zero point foods are constant, the way they are incorporated into your daily eating pattern can be as unique as you are. This allows for personal adjustments and creativity in how these foods are prepared and enjoyed, ensuring that the diet remains a pleasure, not a chore.

Yet, it's crucial to recognize that while zero point foods form the backbone of this system, they are part of a broader, balanced diet. The philosophy does acknowledge the importance of other food groups, including those with healthy fats and denser carbohydrates, which are essential for overall health. These are not eliminated but are advised in mindful proportions, maintaining the holistic balance between managing weight and fueling the body comprehensively.

The implementation of the Zero Point System also places a significant emphasis on other lifestyle factors that influence eating patterns, such as stress management and physical activity. It promotes a lifestyle that supports the dietary changes through managing stress, which often triggers emotional eating, and incorporating moderate physical activity, which is instrumental in maintaining weight loss and overall health.

This approach not only simplifies making healthier choices but integrates them into a broader context of a mindful, balanced lifestyle. It's designed not as a temporary diet but as a sustainable approach to eating that can be adopted for life. The flexibility and focus on overall wellness make the Zero Point System a powerful tool in the arsenal of anyone looking to manage their weight healthily and sustainably.

By following this system, the journey of weight management transforms into a more natural and enjoyable path. It's about making peace with food, understanding its profound role not just in weight loss but in nourishing the body, mind, and spirit. Each meal, each choice becomes an act of self-care, one that respects and celebrates the body's needs, leading to not only a healthier weight but a happier life.

1.3 BENEFITS OF ZERO POINT WEIGHT LOSS

Embracing the Zero Point System is akin to opening a window to a fresh breeze; it's rejuvenating, liberating, and full of potential. The benefits of adopting this method extend far beyond the visible scales of weight loss, impacting a plethora of aspects in one's lifestyle and overall health. This transformation harnesses the power of high-nutrient, low-calorie foods, steering not only towards an optimal weight but also enhancing life quality in several profound ways.

One of the most celebrated advantages of the Zero Point philosophy is the enrichment of dietary quality. Zero point foods are laden with vitamins, minerals, antioxidants, and fibers, all crucial for maintaining robust health. Consuming these nutrient-dense foods regularly can lead to improved nutrition, which naturally fortifies the body's defenses against common ailments and chronic diseases. These foods, from leafy greens to lean proteins, actively contribute to strengthening the immune system, stabilizing blood sugar levels, and reducing inflammation, each step improving overall well-being.

Moreover, weight loss, or more accurately, fat loss, under the Zero Point System is achieved in a manner that preserves muscle mass—a crucial element that many diets overlook. Muscle is metabolically active and plays a significant role in boosting metabolic rate. The inclusion of protein-rich zero point foods ensures that the body is fueled adequately to maintain muscle tissue even as it loses fat, which can significantly enhance the metabolic rate and encourage a more pronounced energy expenditure even during rest.

Another transformative benefit that follows is the regulation of appetite and satiety cues. Zero point foods are rich in fiber and volume, which help fill the stomach and slow digestion. This promotes a longer-lasting sensation of fullness, which naturally curtails overeating and helps in managing calorie intake without the struggle of constant hunger pangs. The mental relief from the cyclical battles of hunger is, in itself, a significant step towards sustainable weight management.

The Zero Point approach also remarkably reduces the cognitive load of dieting. The freedom from counting every calorie, measuring portions precisely, or tracking every bite you eat alleviates stress. This simplicity supports a more relaxed relationship with food, where eating becomes a source of nourishment and joy rather than an exhausting mental exercise fraught with guilt and calculations.

Mental health, an often underappreciated aspect of weight loss regimes, flourishes under the Zero Point plan. With stress reduction and the elimination of restrictive eating patterns, there is often a noted improvement in mood and a decrease in symptoms associated with depression and anxiety. The diet's high content of omega-3 fatty acids, fibers, and antioxidants have known benefits on brain health, which support emotional well-being and enhance cognitive function.

For those with a predisposition to diseases like diabetes and hypertension, the Zero Point System offers a pathway laden with benefits. The dietary fiber in zero point foods plays a crucial role in controlling blood sugar levels, which can vastly improve diabetic conditions. High potassium and low sodium content in these foods also help manage blood pressure levels, thus providing a buffer against hypertension.

Transitioning to family and communal eating, the Zero Point System serves as an excellent model for healthy, communal meals that can be enjoyed by everyone, regardless of their age or health goals. Such practices not only cultivate healthier habits among family members but also strengthen the social bond that shared, mindful eating brings. It becomes a shared journey towards health, improving not just individual wellness but boosting the collective health of communities.

Let's not overlook the long-term sustainability of the Zero Point System. Unlike crash diets that offer rapid weight loss with an equally swift rebound, the Zero Point plan promotes gradual, sustained weight loss that is more likely to last because it's based on making manageable, enjoyable changes to eating habits, rather than imposing ruthless restrictions.

Moreover, environmental consciousness and ethical eating habits also find a place within this approach as zero point foods often include whole, unprocessed items that are less resource-intensive than many processed foods. When chosen wisely, these options can lead to a reduced environmental footprint, adding another layer of benefit to the choice of embracing this lifestyle.

The overall vitality engendered by the Zero Point System can transform lives profoundly. It's not just about losing weight but gaining an enhanced zest for life. Improved physical health leads to improved mental and emotional stability, greater energy levels, and a newfound appreciation for the body's capabilities.

In sum, the decision to adopt the Zero Point System can be likened to opening a gateway to enhanced health and vitality, where eating well becomes not just a diet but a delightful way of life. It's a comprehensive approach that reverberates through every aspect of life, offering a blueprint for not just surviving but thriving.

CHAPTER 2: BUILDING A HEALTHY RELATIONSHIP WITH FOOD

Embarking on a journey toward wellness often means redefining our relationship with the very sustenance that fuels us: food. For many, food is a source of comfort, a medium for celebration, and, at times, a venue for stress. Yet, the heart of sustainable weight loss and vital health lies not just in selecting the right ingredients but in fostering a nurturing connection with what we eat.

Think of your kitchen as a personal wellness sanctuary. As we sift through the pantry or navigate the vibrant aisles of the grocery store, every choice can contribute to an ongoing dialogue with your body. Imagine conversing with each vegetable, grain, and protein source. What would they tell you about the nourishment they provide? How might they help you script a day filled with energy and wellness?

In reacquainting ourselves with the nature of food, we begin to peel back layers of habit and haste, which often obscure mindful eating. It isn't just about swapping out sugar with honey or choosing whole grains over refined ones; it's about understanding the 'why' behind these choices. It's about stopping to savor the burst of a tomato or the zesty tang of a lemon, recognizing each flavor for the masterpiece it is.

Yet, the challenge persists—not just in choosing well but in maintaining these choices amidst a busy schedule and an ever-encroaching world of quick fixes and fast food. Here, the power of preparation and knowledge becomes evident. By understanding the foods that best fuel our unique bodies and learning how to prepare them in quick, delightful ways, we transform our diet from something we have to police into something we are excited to celebrate.

A healthy relationship with food isn't cultivated overnight; it grows from consistent, everyday decisions. It's about making peace with imperfections and learning from each culinary encounter. So, as we move forward, let's embrace this dialogue with open hearts and curious minds, laying down a path towards not just a lighter body, but a richer, more fulfilling life.

2.1 MINDFUL EATING PRACTICES

Mindful eating emerges not only as a practice but as a transformative philosophy in our quest for health and wellness. Beyond the basic act of fueling our bodies, it challenges the rush of our hectic daily routines, urging us to pause and consider what we consume, why we eat it, and how it impacts our feelings and physical sensations.

Envision dining as a daily ritual where each meal unfolds like a narrative that engages all senses. Imagine sitting down with a plate of wholesome food and seeing the array of colors, smelling the enticing aromas, and anticipating the textures against your palate. Mindful eating invites this level of awareness to each dining experience, turning what could be mundane refueling into a moment of genuine pleasure and appreciation.

The concept at the heart of mindful eating is simple: it's about using all senses to engage with food. It's about noticing the colors, the textures, and the flavors, but it's also about tuning into the emotions and physical sensations that accompany eating. This practice helps us recognize our body's hunger and fullness signals, and potentially, it reveals the emotional motivations that urge us to snack when we're not truly hungry.

Lucy, a once-busy marketing executive, shares her transformative journey with mindful eating. Grappling with stress eating and rushed meals, she felt disconnected from the food she consumed, often eating past the point of fullness. Her turning point occurred during a mindful eating workshop where she practiced eating in silence, focusing purely on her meal. Lucy learned to appreciate the sweetness of a strawberry, the crispness of a leaf of lettuce, and even the effort that went into growing and preparing these foods. Slowly, mealtime became an oasis of calm in her chaotic day. This shift didn't just change how she ate; it changed her relationship with food, turning it from a source of guilt into a source of joy and sustenance.

Such stories illuminate the power of mindful eating—it's not just about losing weight or eating 'right'; it's about rediscovering food as a profound source of nourishment.

The process of integrating mindful eating starts with small, manageable steps. Begin by assessing your eating environment. Simplify the space where you eat; a cluttered table can lead to a cluttered mind. Aim for a calm atmosphere where you can sit comfortably and focus on your meal without distractions like TV or smartphones. Next, consider your eating pace. Many of us eat quickly, barely chewing our food. Try to slow down, chewing each bite thoroughly, which aids digestion and allows you to truly taste what you're eating. A helpful method is to place your utensils down between bites—an easy, physical reminder to pause.

Another aspect involves understanding your body's cues. Our bodies have a way of telling us when they need food and when they have had enough. However, in our busy lives, these signals can be easy to overlook or misinterpret. Spend a week tuning into these signals. Before grabbing a snack or sitting down to a meal, ask yourself: Am I really hungry? Or am I bored, stressed, or emotional? After eating, take a moment to note how you feel. Are you comfortably satisfied, or uncomfortably stuffed? Noticing these sensations can prevent overeating and encourage you to eat when you're truly hungry.

For those who eat out of boredom or emotional distress, mindful eating offers a powerful pathway. It encourages us to explore alternatives that can fulfill emotional needs without food, such as taking a walk, reading a book, or practicing deep breathing. This doesn't mean you can't eat when you're stressed, but it invites a moment of pause to consider whether there are other ways to cope.

However, the journey of mindful eating isn't without its hurdles. Distractions are plentiful—from busy family dinners to quick lunches in front of the computer. It might be easier on quieter days than during a stressful week filled with deadlines. Acknowledge these challenges and be gentle with yourself as you navigate them. Each meal is a fresh opportunity to practice mindfulness.

Remember, the essence of mindfulness is non-judgment. As you embark on or continue this practice, notice when judgment arises—whether it's about the food you're choosing, how much you're eating, or how quickly you eat—but gently guide your focus back to your senses and the experience.

As more individuals, like Lucy, embrace mindful eating, a shared narrative unfolds. It tells a story of transformation—a shift from eating mindlessly, governed by habit or emotion, to dining mindfully, with intention and pleasure. It's about more than just the food on the plate; it's about enriching the human experience with each meal, nurturing not just the body, but the soul.

In the end, mindful eating not only enhances your relationship with food but weaves into the broader tapestry of mindful living. By learning to eat mindfully, we learn to live mindfully—aware, present, and profoundly connected to our choices. This not only nourishes our bodies but also our minds, fostering a holistic sense of wellness that reaches far beyond the table.

2.2 OVERCOMING EMOTIONAL EATING

One of the most subtle yet profound challenges on the journey to wellness is understanding and addressing emotional eating. It's a behavior pattern where food serves not as a source of sustenance but as a temporary salve for emotions—be they boredom, stress, sadness, or even celebration. Breaking this pattern involves more than just willpower; it requires a compassionate, insightful approach to redefining the role food plays in our lives.

At its core, emotional eating is not about hunger for food, but hunger for emotional fulfillment. The pantry becomes a go-to place not when the stomach growls but when the heart yearns for comfort, or the mind needs distraction. Consider Sarah, a middle-aged teacher who found herself reaching for chocolate every evening. It wasn't hunger she was trying to satiate; it was stress and loneliness from her demanding job and quiet, empty home. Once she recognized this pattern, she began to explore healthier ways to address her feelings, like evening yoga classes and journaling, which provided genuine comfort without the side effects of sugar.

Understanding emotional eating involves listening deeply to our own stories about food. These narratives often start in childhood and are influenced by how caregivers interacted with food. Did they offer sweets as a reward or consolation? Were there restrictions placed on food that made it feel like a forbidden treasure? Such questions can uncover why food has become tangled with emotion, making it a powerful tool for self-soothing or celebration.

Identifying triggers is another crucial step. Triggers are events or feelings that prompt the automatic reach for comfort food. Common triggers include stress, fatigue, boredom, or social environments. Keeping a food and mood diary can be beneficial here. By documenting not only what and when they eat but also their emotional state, individuals can begin to see patterns, recognizing which feelings tend to push them toward emotional eating.

Once triggers are identified, the next step is developing healthier responses. Instead of immediately gratifying emotional hunger with food, it's about pausing to ask, "What do I really need?" This question can redirect the impulsive energy to more fulfilling answers. Maybe what's needed is a conversation with a friend, some fresh air, or a few moments of meditation. These alternatives address emotional needs without the repercussions of unwanted calories.

But developing new habits is not an overnight fix. It requires consistent practice. One method is the "Five-Minute Rule." When the urge to eat emotionally strikes, set a timer for five minutes. During this time, engage in a different, preferably enjoyable, activity. If, after five minutes, the urge to eat persists, allow yourself a small portion of what you're craving in a mindful, controlled manner. This practice can help reshape the rush from emotional discomfort into mindful decision-making.

It's also vital to learn how to be comfortable with emotions, without rushing to smother them with food. Emotional resilience can be built by allowing feelings to surface and addressing them head-on. Techniques such as deep breathing, mindfulness meditation, or speaking with a therapist can equip individuals with tools to cope with emotions in healthier ways.

In Sarah's case, adopting these strategies was transformative. By identifying her triggers and developing healthier responses, she gradually found emotional eating to be a less frequent compulsion. Instead, emotional resilience became her new norm. She learned to derive joy from yoga and fulfillment from journaling, effectively breaking her dependence on chocolate for comfort.

Furthermore, fostering a balanced lifestyle that includes adequate sleep, regular physical activity, and strong social connections can preempt the conditions often leading to emotional eating. Sleep deprivation, lack of physical activity, and social isolation can heighten emotional vulnerability and make reaching for comfort food more likely.

Ultimately, overcoming emotional eating is a journey toward deeper self-understanding and self-care. It's about establishing a sustainable relationship with food where eating becomes a response to physical hunger more so than emotional distress. This doesn't mean emotions shouldn't play a role in our eating experiences—celebratory meals, consolatory coffees, joyous gatherings around food are all beautiful aspects of human culture. The goal is balance, not abstinence; harmony, not control.

As individuals learn to meet their emotional needs without food, they gain not only a healthier body but also a more wholesome and fulfilling life. Emotional eating, once a shadow over their relationship with food, can become a doorway to a deeper understanding of their own needs and desires, turning their journey into a story of transformation and empowerment. It's about changing the narrative from eating to comfort oneself to eating to nourish oneself—both body and spirit.

2.3 Setting Realistic and Sustainable Goals

Embarking on a wellness journey often begins with a burst of motivation and a long list of goals. However, as the days pass, these ambitious milestones can sometimes feel overwhelming or unrealistic, leading to frustration and discouragement. To truly succeed in building a healthy relationship with food, it's essential to set goals that are not only achievable but also sustainable and aligned with your lifestyle and values.

Consider the story of Mark, who initially set a goal to lose 30 pounds in three months. Despite his initial enthusiasm, he quickly found himself slipping into old habits, feeling overwhelmed by the drastic changes he thought necessary to achieve his goal. It was only after reassessing his approach and setting smaller, more manageable goals that Mark began to see success. He focused on making one healthy change at a time, such as incorporating more vegetables into his meals or reducing his intake of processed foods, which eventually led to lasting weight loss and a more peaceful relationship with food.

Setting realistic and sustainable goals involves a process of careful consideration and self-reflection. Start by asking yourself what you truly want to achieve from your dietary changes. Is your aim to feel more energized, to improve your health metrics, or perhaps to be a role model for healthy eating within your family? Clarifying your objectives will help guide the goals you set and ensure they align with your broader life aspirations.

Once your objectives are clear, the next step is to break them into specific, measurable, achievable, relevant, and time-bound (SMART) goals. For instance, rather than having a vague goal like "eat healthier," a SMART goal would be, "I will include at least one serving of leafy greens in my lunch five days a week for the next month." This method not only defines what success looks like but also provides a clear timeline for evaluation. Meeting these smaller goals provides a sense of accomplishment which fuels further motivation. Each minor victory is a building block towards larger, long-term goals, making the process less daunting and more enjoyable. It's also crucial to anticipate potential barriers. Life's unpredictable nature can sometimes disrupt even the best plans. Understanding these challenges and developing strategies to overcome them, whether it's prepping meals in advance or finding healthy take-out options for busy nights, can prevent setbacks and keep you on track.

One effective strategy for maintaining motivation is to keep a record of your progress. Whether it's a journal, a mobile app, or simply a calendar where you check off goals as you achieve them, seeing the progress visually can be a powerful motivator. Besides, this documentation can help identify patterns or triggers that lead to less healthy eating habits, which you can then address proactively.

Another crucial aspect is flexibility. While discipline is important, being too rigid can make a healthy eating plan feel like a chore rather than a lifestyle change. Allowing yourself occasional treats or indulgences can make your goals feel more achievable and prevent the feelings of deprivation that might otherwise sabotage your success.

It's also important to surround yourself with support. Sharing your goals with friends, family, or a support group can not only provide encouragement but also accountability. Having someone to share your challenges and successes with can make the journey less intimidating and more enjoyable.

Moreover, it's vital to celebrate successes, no matter how small. Every step forward is a step in the right direction. Celebrating these achievements can boost your confidence and reinforce your commitment to your health goals.

Finally, be patient and kind to yourself. Change doesn't happen overnight. There will be good days and bad days, successes and setbacks. The key is to stay focused on why you started and to treat each new day as an opportunity to reinforce your healthy habits.

By setting realistic and thoughtful goals, you not only set the stage for achievable success but also integrate these changes into your life in a way that feels natural and sustainable. This approach ensures that your relationship with food is not about restriction but about enhancement — enhancing your health, your mood, and your overall quality of life, one meal at a time.

CHAPTER 3: NAVIGATING COMMON DIETARY CHALLENGES

Every journey encounters its share of roadblocks, and the path to sustaining a healthy diet is no exception. Imagine you are navigating a city for the first time without a map; undoubtedly, you might take a few wrong turns. The dietary world is much the same, filled with complex food labels, stressful social dining, and the pervasive temptation of comfort eating when you've had a long day.

In Chapter 3, we address some of the most common dietary challenges that you might face along your weight loss journey. The goal is not only to recognize these roadblocks but also to equip you with strategic detours and shortcuts to keep you on the right path.

Let's take a moment to explore stress eating—a familiar detour for many. It's the end of a long, demanding day at work, and all you crave is that cheesy pizza because, honestly, it feels like a warm hug for your overworked soul. Here, it's crucial to apply a mindful approach, one where you acknowledge the craving but also arm yourself with healthier, yet equally satisfying alternatives. Think of a steaming bowl of zucchini noodle pasta topped with marinara and a sprinkle of nutritional yeast. Doesn't that sound comforting and inviting?

Then, there's the social gathering dilemma. Picture this: you're at a birthday party where the table is laden with sugary desserts, greasy snacks, and not a single food item that fits your wellness plan. Instead of succumbing to the pressure or isolating yourself, you could become an advocate for your health, perhaps by collaborating with the host ahead of time to include some dishes that everyone, including you, can enjoy guilt-free.

Through these scenarios and more, this chapter is designed to transform your potential stumbling blocks into stepping stones. Each challenge is an opportunity to reinforce your commitment to a healthier you, making you not just a follower of a diet, but a leader in your own life's journey. So let's take this step-by-step, learning to navigate through dietary dilemmas with poise and confidence. Together, we'll keep your wellness goals not just within sight, but well within reach.

3.1 Balancing Zero Point Foods with Other Nutrients

Understanding how to balance zero point foods with other necessary nutrients represents one of the more intricate aspects of sustaining a wholesome diet while pursuing weight loss. For those unfamiliar, zero point foods are those that you can eat without measuring every bite or stressing over calories—fruits, most vegetables, and lean proteins, for example. They make up the backbone of a flexible and maintainable dietary plan. However, the real puzzle lies not just in enjoying these foods but in integrating them skillfully with other essential nutrients to maintain overall health.

Think of your diet as a vibrant tapestry, each thread representing different food groups and nutrients, interwoven to create a harmonious and functional whole. Relying too heavily on zero point foods can skew this tapestry, leaving it unbalanced. It's akin to playing a beautiful melody with only a few notes; while it might sound sweet for a time, the complexity and richness of the composition will be lacking.

To paint a clearer picture, consider protein—one of the building blocks of your body. While lean meats might classify as zero point foods, it's crucial to also look at sources that might carry a few more points, such as fatty fishes like salmon, rich in omega-3 fatty acids, which are vital for cardiovascular health. This highlights the necessity of looking beyond the point system to the broader nutritional value foods offer.

Additionally, whole grains and legumes, though costlier in points, are invaluable. They provide a myriad of benefits from fibers that aid digestion and keep you feeling full longer, to essential minerals. Including a serving of quinoa or black beans in your meals ensures a sustained release of energy, which helps in managing appetite and reducing binge-eating tendencies.

Then, there is the matter of dietary fats, commonly misunderstood as a nemesis in weight loss journeys. However, fats like those from avocados, nuts, and seeds are crucial for your body's nutrient absorption and neurological health. These foods might carry more points, but excluding them can deprive your body of these necessary benefits. It's much like leaving colors out of your painting; the result might fulfill some purpose but won't hold the same value or beauty.

A common pitfall when focusing too intensely on zero point foods is the potential neglect of micronutrients—vitamins and minerals that don't inherently contribute calories but play critical roles in functions ranging from bone health to immune function. Consider iron, which is pivotal for energy as it's integral in the making of hemoglobin, the protein responsible for transporting oxygen in your blood. Lean red meats, often higher in points than chicken, are excellent sources of iron. Therefore, incorporating measured portions of these can prevent deficiencies that might leave you feeling unexpectedly fatigued or weak, undermining your diet and daily productivity.

Balancing this intricate web of nutrition might seem daunting, reminiscent of juggling too many balls in the air. Yet, like any skill, it improves with practice and patience. Start by viewing your meals through the lens of diversity—aim for color and variety, ensuring that you're pulling nutrients from across the spectrum.

One practical approach is to plan your meals ahead. This isn't about restriction but rather about preparation. When you plan, you have the clarity to ensure that each meal is balanced, combining zero point foods with others that contribute essential fats, proteins, and carbohydrates. Furthermore, this reduces the daily stress of decision-making—a significant psychological benefit.

Another useful strategy is to educate yourself about the nutritional content of foods, especially those that are not zero points. Knowledge is power, and understanding what each food brings to your table empowers you to make informed choices, thus enforcing a diet plan that transcends mere points and deeply nourishes your body. Remember, the aim here is not perfection but progress. Balancing your foods effectively means giving your body all the instruments it needs to play the symphony of day-to-day life with vitality and vigor. It's about making peace with the scale, not letting it dictate every food choice, thereby encouraging a relationship with food that is based on nourishment rather than numbers alone.

In essence, the journey through dietary challenges, particularly in balancing zero point foods with others, is much like navigating a river. There will be smooth stretches and rough rapids. The key is to steer with knowledge and adaptability, using your understanding as your compass, guiding you towards sustained wellness and health. By recognizing and respecting the role of various nutrients in your diet, you can ensure that your nutritional intake is as rich and varied as the life you wish to lead. This balanced approach allows you to enjoy the journey of weight loss and health management without feeling deprived or sidelined by dietary restrictions. It's about embracing the full spectrum of foods, each playing its unique part in your health and wellness journey.

3.2 Managing Portion Sizes and Serving Suggestions

In the landscape of healthy eating and weight management, the significance of portion sizes and serving suggestions cannot be overstated. It's akin to the art of filling a canvas; too much paint can overwhelm the details, just as too little might fail to express the full picture. The same applies to how we serve our meals: too much and we risk overindulgence; too little, and we may not be nourishing our bodies adequately.

The challenge often lies in distinguishing how much is just right—especially in a society where portion sizes have quietly expanded over the years. A plate piled high at a restaurant often carries double, sometimes triple, the amount recommended for a single serving. This cultural norm can distort our perception of what is appropriate, subtly influencing how we serve ourselves at home.

Consider the serene process of a sculptor, carefully measuring and removing excess to reveal the perfect form. Managing portion sizes requires a similar precision and mindfulness. It involves understanding the bodies' needs and responding thoughtfully, rather than reacting out of habit or compulsion.

Begin with a grounding in what constitutes a serving size. Visual cues can be surprisingly effective. For instance, envision a deck of cards; this is roughly the size of a recommended serving of meat. A cupped hand holds about half a cup of pasta or rice, about right for a single serving. Such comparisons are handy checks that prevent over-service at meal times without the need for scales or measuring cups, seamlessly integrating into the flow of daily life.

Integration of this awareness into meals involves a blend of mindfulness and strategy. It starts at the grocery store. Shopping with a list prevents impulse buys of bulk items that might tempt one to overeat. At home, using smaller plates can naturally encourage smaller servings without a sense of deprivation—a psychological trick that harnesses perception to serve wellness.

Another effective method is the division of food into portions before it's served. When cooking a meal, immediately allocate the leftovers into containers for future lunches or dinners. This not only manages portion size but also simplifies meal planning for the week, addressing both health and efficiency.

Engaging more deeply with your hunger cues forms the crux of portion control. Before reaching for a second helping, pause. It takes about 20 minutes for the stomach to signal to the brain that it's full. Use this interlude to converse with fellow diners, savor the meal's flavors, or drink a glass of water. Often, you might find that the initial impulse to eat more ebbs away, leaving you comfortably satisfied with the first serving.

In managing portion sizes at home, empowerment comes from education. Educate yourself and, if applicable, your family, about the sizes of servings. Make it a shared journey; perhaps hold a 'serving size' quiz night where you compare guessed portions to actual recommended amounts. Such activities embed knowledge in a fun yet impactful manner, helping to recalibrate perceptions and habits around food.

Aside from managing portion sizes at home, dining out presents its challenges. Here, strategy shifts from control to negotiation. Begin by reviewing the menu online beforehand to make mindful choices free from the pressure of the moment. Once at the restaurant, consider ordering a single entrée to share or choosing an appetizer as a main dish. If larger portions are unavoidable, request a box at the start of the meal to set aside the excess before you begin eating. This removes the temptation to nibble beyond fullness just because food remains on the plate. The journey to mastering portion control is akin to tuning an instrument, each adjustment improving the harmony it brings to your life. It requires constant, mindful engagement with your eating habits and proactive strategies to maintain balance. Over time, these practices can reshape your relationship with food, leading not only to weight loss but also to a more intuitive, satisfying approach to eating.

In essence, managing portion sizes is less about restrictive metrics and more about cultivating a self-aware relationship with food. By nurturing this connection, you ensure that every meal nourishes not just the body but also the mind, aligning with the overarching themes of balance and wellness that define a healthy, sustainable lifestyle. This is how you reclaim control, not just of your diet, but of your holistic health, transforming eating from a mundane daily necessity to a source of daily joy and balance.

3.3 Eating Out and Social Events: Staying on Track

Navigating the social seas of dining out and attending events while maintaining your wellness goals is akin to walking a tightrope. It requires balance, focus, and, most importantly, a strategy that respects both your social life and your health commitments.

Picture this: you're at a joyous wedding, surrounded by friends, family, and tempting dishes at every turn. Or perhaps you're at a dinner gathering where the table is laden with your favorite foods, ones you've mastered the art of avoiding in your day-to-day routine. It's not just the food that's the challenge, but the emotional, celebratory environment that makes you want to indulge as part of the experience.

The key to maintaining control in these situations lies in preparation and mindset adjustment—strategies that align with our previous discussions about mindfulness and portion control, yet tailored to address the unique challenges presented by social settings.

Preparation is Your Friend

Just as a skilled sailor studies the weather before setting sail, a smart diner prepares for a meal out. This could involve perusing the menu online to make informed choices beforehand, thus avoiding snap decisions made under the social pressure or influence of hunger. Opt for dishes that are grilled, steamed, or baked—cooking methods that typically imply less fat and calories than their fried or creamy counterparts.

Another practical tactic involves eating a small, nutritious snack before attending an event. A piece of fruit, a small yogurt, or a handful of nuts can curb your hunger, affording you more control when you face the buffet. This is not just about physical satiety, but psychological readiness; you're less likely to feel deprived and therefore less tempted to overeat.

Setting the Mental Stage

Once you arrive at the event, it's crucial to shift your focus away from the food and towards the people and the celebration. Food is just one part of the event, not the centerpiece. Engage in conversations, participate in activities, and immerse yourself in the joyous occasion rather than hovering around the buffet or snack table.

When it's time to eat, visualize your plate as a canvas. Lean proteins, vegetables, and a wholesome carb source can create a balanced, colorful meal. This technique not only helps in selecting your meal but also serves as a reminder of how far you've come in your journey towards mindful eating.

Navigating Choices

When confronted with multiple food options, prioritize dishes that are closest to what you'd eat at home. It's also helpful to fill your plate only once to avoid the temptation of going back for seconds. If you do wish to try a bit of everything, consider the 'three-bite rule'—savoring three small bites of a decadent dish to satisfy your curiosity without going overboard.

Social gatherings often involve alcohol, which can be both a calorie trap and a catalyst for losing dietary restraint. Opting for sparkling water, a light spritzer, or simply setting a limit to the number of alcoholic beverages can help maintain your dietary boundaries while still participating in the toast.

When to Bend

Flexibility is essential, especially in maintaining a balanced perspective on diet and life. If there's a special dish that you love, allow yourself the flexibility to enjoy it. The goal is not to create a rigid framework but to foster a sustainable lifestyle where occasional indulgences are neither disastrous nor causes for guilt.

After the Event

Post-event, it's important to reflect on your experiences. Assess what strategies worked, what didn't, and how you felt during the event. This reflective practice not only reinforces positive behaviors but also prepares you better for future scenarios.

Also, it's crucial to return to your regular eating habits the next day. One celebration meal does not derail your progress, just as one good meal doesn't guarantee health. It's the consistent, mindful choices that make the journey toward wellness sustainable.

Eating out and attending social events while maintaining a diet are part of the broader challenge of integrating a healthy lifestyle into a vibrant, active social life. It's about making peace with the landscape of social dining by preparing adequately, making informed choices, focusing on the social aspect of gatherings, and forgiving yourself when you stray from the plan. With these strategies, each event becomes not just an occasion to celebrate with loved ones but also an opportunity to practice and reinforce your commitment to a healthier, more balanced you. In integrating these practices, you navigate your social and culinary environments with grace and poise, making your diet a natural part of your vibrant lifestyle rather than an obstacle to enjoying life's great moments.

CHAPTER 4: PRACTICAL MEAL PLANNING STRATEGIES

Imagine you've just finished a long day at work, and now you're standing in the grocery store aisle, utterly exhausted. Your mind is wrestling with a series of questions: What should I cook? How can I whip up something quick yet healthy? It is moments like these, when time ticks loudly and your energy dwindles, that the benefits of having a meal plan sparkle like a beacon of hope.

In Chapter 4, we're diving into the art of practical meal planning—your secret weapon for sustaining your wellness and weight loss goals with ease and efficiency. Think of meal planning not as a strict regimen but as creating a weekly playlist of your favorite tunes; it's personal, flexible, and tuned to your life's rhythm.

Let's paint a picture of tomorrow with meal planning in the frame. Imagine waking up knowing exactly what's on the menu for breakfast, lunch, and dinner. No last-minute decisions, no unhealthy take-outs. Instead, you have a fridge stocked with prepped ingredients that can be turned into delicious, nutritious meals in no time. This isn't just a time-saver; it's a stress reducer and a health booster.

Now, picture this scenario enhanced with our zero point food system, where the focus is on nutrient-dense, low-calorie foods that can be eaten in abundant quantities. Meal planning with this system allows you to assemble meals ahead of time that are not only healthy but are also bursting with flavor. It means less thinking and more enjoying.

Throughout this chapter, we will explore strategies to integrate meal planning into your routine, no matter how hectic it may seem. From choosing the right recipes to understanding portion sizes, you'll discover how to streamline your cooking processes, reduce waste, and maintain flavor without compromising nutritional value. Reinventing your meal preparation approach will transform your daily life, freeing up time that can be spent enjoying the company of loved ones or simply unwinding. It's about making mealtime an eagerly anticipated part of your day, not a daunting task. So, let's embark on this journey towards a more organized, flavorful, and health-forward lifestyle.

4.1 Efficient Grocery Shopping Tips

Stepping into the grocery store can sometimes feel like entering a battlefield. You're faced with endless choices, tempting treats calling your name, and the overwhelming pressure to stick to your wellness goals while staying on budget. However, your grocery shopping doesn't have to be a stressful ordeal. With some strategic thinking and efficient planning, it can transform into an enjoyable part of your healthy lifestyle. This sub-chapter aims to turn your grocery shopping into an efficient, fulfilling experience that supports your weight loss and wellness journey.

The first step towards efficient grocery shopping begins much before you even step foot in the store. It starts right at your home, preparing a well-thought-out shopping list. But this isn't just any list; this is your blueprint for the week ahead. Consider your meal plan, which you've developed from the previous discussions on practical meal planning, and list out all the ingredients you need. This method not only saves time wandering down aisles but also prevents impulse buys that can derail your diet.

As you prepare your list, categorize items based on their location in the store. Most grocery stores are laid out with perishables like fruits and vegetables at one end and frozen goods at another. Start with the produce section and end with the frozen items to ensure that your perishable goods don't spend too much time at room temperature. By mapping your route through the grocery store, you minimize backtracking and reduce the temptation to wander into the snack aisle.

Speaking of produce, let's delve into choosing the right fruits and vegetables. Focus on seasonal produce; these are not only cheaper but also at their nutrient peak. However, the real secret here is to also consider versatility—select vegetables and fruits that can be used in multiple meals. For example, bell peppers can be snipped into salads, stir-fried, or filled and baked. This approach minimizes waste and gives you more bang for your buck.

Now, onto one of the biggest challenges: managing costs without compromising on quality. One effective strategy is to embrace the bulk section for dry goods like nuts, seeds, and grains. Buying in bulk can often be more economical and allows you to purchase the exact quantities you need, which again reduces waste. Also, be on the lookout for sales and promotions, but be cautious—only buy what fits into your meal plan. Stocking up on sale items that you don't need can lead to overeating or wasted food.

Another money-saving trick involves embracing store brands. Many store-brand products are manufactured by the same companies that produce higher-priced, name-brand items and are nearly identical in quality. This simple switch can shave significant amounts from your grocery bill without sacrificing quality.

When it comes to meat and fish, consider less expensive cuts. With the right preparation techniques, such as marinating or slow cooking, these can be just as delicious as their pricey counterparts. Moreover, consider incorporating one or two vegetarian meals per week. Plant-based proteins like lentils, beans, and chickpeas are cost-effective, nutritious, and can be used in a variety of dishes.

Preserving the freshness of what you buy is also crucial. Invest time in properly storing foods when you get home. For example, wrap leafy greens in paper towels to absorb excess moisture before bagging them, which can help extend their life. Understanding and implementing proper storage techniques ensures that your groceries maintain their quality as long as possible, reducing the amount of food that might otherwise go to waste.

Lastly, while efficiency is key, it's also important to make grocery shopping a pleasant experience. Perhaps you can turn it into a learning activity by bringing your children along and teaching them about nutrition. Or treat the time to explore new food options as a mini-adventure, sampling one new fruit or vegetable each week. This not only broadens your dietary horizons but also keeps the excitement in your meal plan.

Efficient grocery shopping isn't just about saving time and money; it's about making choices that enhance your health, fit your lifestyle, and bring joy into your meal preparation. By shopping smart, you uphold your commitment to a healthy, balanced lifestyle without letting it become a chore. Next time you grab that shopping cart, you're not just filling it with food; you're stocking up on the foundations of your continued health and well-being. So, embrace these tips and transform your grocery shopping from a mundane task into a cornerstone of your wellness journey.

4.2 Meal Prep Techniques for Busy Lifestyles

Meal prep is like the quietly efficient friend who's always there to help you through the busiest days. Imagine drawing the curtains on Sunday evening, the kitchen filled with the aroma of your well-planned dinners for the week, and the calming assurance that no matter how chaotic the upcoming days might be, your meals are sorted. This might sound like a distant dream when you're stuck in weekly grind, but with some clever meal prep techniques tailored for busy lifestyles, this can be very much your reality.

Firstly, let's view meal prep as more than just a time-saving tactic; see it as an essential puzzle piece in your wellness journey. The process involves selecting a day to prepare multiple meals at once, usually for the week ahead. This method streamlines your eating habits, curbs the temptation of unplanned indulgences, and aligns perfectly with our zero point food system where the emphasis lies on healthful, low-calorie, nutrient-dense foods.

When embarking on your meal prep adventure, start by selecting recipes that hold up well over a few days and can be easily multiplied. Dishes like hearty veggie casseroles, lean protein stir-fries, and robust salads (dressed on the day of eating) are great choices. The trick is to cook once, eat multiple times, without the meals getting mundane.

Segmenting meals into individual portions is your next step. This not only controls portion sizes, assisting in effective weight management, but it also makes it incredibly easy to grab your meals on the go. Invest in good-quality, durable food storage containers that stack neatly in your fridge, are microwavable, and some that are even stylish enough to be taken directly to the dining table.

Efficiency in meal prep often comes down to strategic cooking sequences. Start with foods that take the longest to cook like whole grains or baked dishes, while simultaneously prepping vegetables or quick-cooks like stir-fries. Also, consider recipes that utilize the same ingredients in different ways. A batch of quinoa can be a side for a grilled salmon on Tuesday and transform into a quinoa salad with mixed vegetables on Thursday.

Another technique is the smart use of kitchen gadgets. Slow cookers, pressure cookers, and even air fryers can significantly cut down your active kitchen time. A slow cooker can simmer your chili while you're at work; a pressure cooker can make a pulpy mix for soups in minutes, and an air fryer can churn out crispy veggies without you having to hover near the stove.

Amidst these preparations, don't forget the flexibility factor. Sometimes, life throws a curveball, and you might need to adjust your meals. Having a few backup solutions, like quick recipes or healthy freezer-friendly meals ready to go, can keep you on track without stress. Adjustability also means leaving room to listen to your body's cravings and providing options within your meal plan to accommodate these hunger nudges without falling off the wagon.

Then there's the delicate matter of balancing variety with consistency. While it's efficient to eat the same meal multiple times, boredom can set in. To combat this while still keeping prep simple, alter the flavors with different herbs, spices, or simple sides. Consider toggling between steamed and roasted vegetables or changing up the sauces and seasonings in dishes to keep your taste buds intrigued.

Lastly, remember that meal prep is an evolving process. It needs to adapt to your changing schedule, preferences, and nutritional needs. Occasionally, take a step back to re-evaluate what's working and what's not. Maybe you've discovered new ingredients that simplify preparation even more, or perhaps your household's taste preferences have shifted.

Meal prep isn't just chopping and cooking in bulk. It's about crafting a sustainable approach to eating that supports your lifestyle without compromising on taste or health—much like curating a personal menu that lives in your fridge, ready to go whenever you are. Turn those Sunday prep sessions into a ritual that sets the tone for a week of eating well, living well, and embracing the chaos of busy days with one less thing to worry about. Drawing from your store of readily available, healthy meals keeps you empowered and energized, no matter what your week throws at you.

4.3 Creating Balanced and Satisfying Meals

Creating meals that nourish the body and delight the senses is an art infused with a touch of practical wisdom. For those endeavoring to lose weight and uplift their health, the artistry lies in crafting meals that are not only balanced and satisfying but also maintain interest and enjoyment over time. This integral component of your wellness journey compels you to think beyond mere calorie counts and nutrient quotas—it invites you to weave a tapestry of flavors and textures that transform regular dining into a celebration of wholesome living.

In understanding how to construct such well-rounded meals, it's essential to first appreciate the foundational elements of nutrition—carbohydrates, proteins, fats, vitamins, and minerals—all playing unique roles in maintaining bodily functions and boosting energy levels. The key to a satisfying meal lies in its balance, ensuring that each of these nutrients is present in the right proportions. This balance not only optimizes health benefits but also enhances the meal's ability to satiate, providing a lasting feeling of fullness and contentment.

A balanced meal starts with a generous base of vegetables, which are high in fiber and rich in vitamins and minerals while being low in calories. This ensures volume without the caloric overload, a critical point for those tracking weight loss. From vibrant leafy greens to crunchy carrots, the options are vast and varied. Integrating a variety of colors and textures not only enriches the meal's nutritional profile but also enhances its visual allure, making it more appetizing and enjoyable.

Protein is the next cornerstone, vital for its role in muscle repair and growth. Options range from lean meats and fish to plant-based choices like lentils, beans, and tofu. The trick is to vary protein sources across meals to prevent monotony and to supply the body with a broad spectrum of amino acids, the building blocks of proteins. Carbohydrates, often misunderstood and unnecessarily feared, are actually pivotal for energy. Whole grains like quinoa, brown rice, and whole wheat pasta provide sustained energy, as opposed to the short spikes offered by their refined counterparts. They also contribute to the feeling of fullness and should be included mindfully within each meal.

Fats, though calorie-dense, are essential for nutrient absorption and brain health. Incorporating healthy fats through avocados, nuts, seeds, or olive oil can significantly uplift the meal's flavor profile and satiety level while fostering long-term health benefits.

However, a truly satisfying meal transcends the mere checklist of nutrients. It involves the delicate interplay of flavors and textures, which can transform an ordinary meal into an extraordinary dining experience. Imagine the crunch of seeds, the smoothness of well-cooked legumes, the sharpness of a vinaigrette, or the subtle sweetness from a piece of fruit—all these elements play in harmony to create a fulsome mouthfeel and layered flavors.

Besides the physiological aspects, the psychological dimensions of creating balanced and satisfying meals also hold water. Consider the comfort derived from a warm bowl of soup on a chilly evening or the invigorating freshness of a summer salad. Meals should be contextual, aligning with the body's needs and the soul's cravings, dictated by season, weather, and mood.

Meal planning, in this pursuit, is not just a tool for organizing but an act of mindfulness. It requires envisioning the week's needs based on your schedule, physical demands, and emotional state. Some days might call for more hearty, comforting meals if they follow intense physical or mental exertion, while others might need lighter, refreshing foods.

Let's not forget the role of simplicity and time efficiency which is paramount, especially for those juggling multiple responsibilities. Recipes that reuse ingredients in creative ways or techniques that decrease active cooking time without compromising quality serve as invaluable hacks for maintaining consistency in your meal preparation.

Lastly, while the act of eating is individual, the joy of food is often magnified by sharing. Meals that are adaptable to different dietary preferences and can be enjoyed by the whole family not only reduce the cook's burden but also enhance the communal joy of eating. This shared experience can reinforce relationships, create lasting memories, and establish healthy eating habits across generations.

Thus, the creation of balanced and satisfying meals is not just about nutrition—it's about crafting an enriching experience that supports your body, delights your palate, and harmonizes with your lifestyle. Each meal then becomes a stepping stone towards a more fulfilled and healthier life, painting your wellness journey with broad strokes of vibrant flavors, varied textures, and invaluable joy.

CHAPTER 5: INTEGRATING HEALTHY HABITS INTO YOUR DAILY ROUTINE

Imagine you're starting your day with a sense of tranquility and purpose, despite the familiar hustle and bustle that awaits you. This isn't just a rare morning of zen-like calm, but the new norm you're gradually building through simple, yet profoundly impactful, healthy habits. In this chapter, we will explore how you can weave these habits seamlessly into the rhythm of your daily life, turning what once felt like a juggling act into a graceful dance.

Each day offers us a canvas, and while we can't always control the colors life throws at us, we can choose how to blend them. Let's say, for instance, you have only ten minutes in the morning before the chaos kicks in. Those precious minutes could be your gateway to a day lived with greater intention and health. Picture this: while your coffee brews, you stretch gently, filling your lungs with deep, nourishing breaths, setting a serene tone for the day. With time, this small practice could well evolve into your non-negotiable morning ritual, much like brushing your teeth.

Now, integrate this approach into meal times which, for many, are often rushed or skipped altogether. What if you could transform even a quick lunch into an opportunity for mindful eating? It's about savoring each bite and truly experiencing the flavors, which not only enhances your dining experience but also signals to your body when you're satisfactorily full, thereby averting the likelihood of overeating.

As we delve deeper, we also consider those often inevitable mid-afternoon slumps. A simple five-minute walk or some quick stretches at your desk can revitalize your senses more effectively than any caffeine fix could. This isn't about adding more to your already full plate; rather, it's about enriching your daily routine in ways that make everything else more manageable and enjoyable.

By the end of this chapter, you'll see that integrating healthy habits into your daily routine is less about making drastic changes and more about making a series of small, deliberate choices that collectively lead to a balanced, energized life. Together, these choices form a mosaic of wellness that not only brightens your days but also sets a positive example for those around you. So, let's start this journey together, one simple step at a time.

5.1 Incorporating Physical Activity

Just as the morning sun gently unravels the dark, incorporating physical activity into your routine can illuminate and transform your whole day. Think of Emma, a software developer who spent hours at her desk, wondering how she could possibly weave some exercise into her packed schedule. Her story is like many of yours—it begins with a challenge and evolves into a triumphant journey of finding wellness in motion.

Emma started with something as manageable as walking. Instead of the typical scene at lunch, rushing through a meal at her desk, she decided to spend the first ten minutes of her lunch break walking around the block. Initially, it was less about fitness and more about clearing her mind. However, she quickly found that these brief strolls not just cleared her head but also energized her for the second part of her day. From there, her walks became longer, and the habit stuck—rain or shine.

This isn't just about Emma or about walking; this is about finding ways to incorporate physical activity that resonate with your life. Physical activity needn't be framed as an "all-or-nothing" mission; it's an accessible path to improving both your physical and mental health, one step at a time.

Rediscover the Joy of Movement

You don't have to relive your high school gym classes to get moving. It starts with reconnecting with the innate joy of movement that we all harbored as children. Remember those days when running around outside wasn't just exercise, but a form of play? Bring back some of that joy. Dance while you clean, stretch during TV commercials, or take a walking meeting at work instead of sitting in a conference room.

Make it a Habit

The key to making physical activity a part of your life is turning it into a habit. For many, the thought of establishing a new habit might sound daunting. However, if you start small and link your new activity to an existing routine, it becomes much easier. For example, after dropping your kids off at school, park a little further away and take a few minutes to walk. Or commit to a quick 10-minute workout right after brushing your teeth in the morning. These small increments can subtly merge into your lifestyle, becoming as routine as your morning coffee.

Optimize Your Environment

Your environment plays a significant role in fostering an active lifestyle. Organize your living space in a way that encourages movement. Keep your yoga mat rolled out in your living room to invite a quick session. Have a kettlebell or jump rope nearby for easy access. If you spend a lot of time at a desk, consider a standing desk or a desk cycle. By integrating physical tools into your living space, you're more likely to use them.

Involve Your Community

Incorporating others into your activity regimen can be a game changer. Not only does it make the process more enjoyable, but it also adds a layer of accountability that can increase your commitment. It could be as simple as a weekly hike with a friend or joining a local community sports league. When you share your activities with others, the social interaction can enhance the emotional benefits of exercise, making it something you look forward to rather than a chore.

Listen to Your Body

One crucial aspect often overlooked is the importance of tuning into your body's signals. Exercise should not be a punishment. If you're feeling exhausted or experiencing pain, give yourself permission to adapt your activities or take a break. It's all about nurturing your body, not breaking it down.

Celebrate Progress, No Matter How Small

Every step, every stretch, every dance move contributes to your wellbeing. Celebrate your willingness to incorporate this movement, however minor it might seem. These aren't just physical feats; they're mental victories over the inertia of a sedentary lifestyle.

Remain Adaptable

Your physical routine will need to evolve just as your life does. Be open to changing your activities based on changing interests, seasons, or physical conditions. What worked for you last year might not fit this year, and that's completely fine. Flexibility in your approach can help sustain physical activity as a permanent part of your life rather than a phase.

Reflect on the Benefits

As you integrate more activity into your life, take time to observe and reflect on how it affects you. Maybe you notice more energy, better sleep, or a more joyful mood. These reflections can reinforce the value of physical activity, motivating you to continue.

Through Emma's story and the practical steps outlined here, I hope you see that adding more physical activity into your daily routine doesn't have to be an upheaval. It can be a smooth, enjoyable enhancement to your life, paving the way not just for weight management, but for a happier, healthier you. Remember, every bit of movement counts in your journey to wellbeing, bringing light and energy into your everyday experiences.

5.2 STRESS MANAGEMENT AND SELF-CARE PRACTICES

In the midst of our fast-paced lives, stress has become a frequent, unwelcome guest, quietly impacting our health, mood, and overall well-being. However, its ubiquitous presence doesn't mean we are powerless. Through thoughtful stress management and self-care practices, we have the tools not only to cope but to thrive even in the face of daily pressures. Let's explore how to transform stress from a formidable foe into a manageable part of our lives.

Imagine Sarah, a project manager and a mother of two, who found herself grappling with the constant demands of her career and family life. The stress was palpable, affecting her sleep, her mood, and her ability to be present with her children. Her story reflects a common narrative, but it's how she rewrote her script on dealing with stress that provides both inspiration and a guide.

Understanding Stress

Firstly, understanding what triggers your stress is critical. For Sarah, it was the fear of not meeting deadlines and the constant juggle between work and parenting. Recognizing these triggers helped her approach her stress points more objectively. It's helpful to mentally note what specific aspects of your day or your environment elevate your stress levels.

Mindfulness and Meditation

One of the most powerful tools for managing stress is developing a practice of mindfulness or meditation. These practices anchor you in the present moment, often reducing the overwhelm that comes from worrying about the future or ruminating over the past. Sarah incorporated short, five-minute meditation sessions into her morning routine. This small practice brought a significant shift in her ability to handle stress throughout the day. The beauty of mindfulness and meditation is that they require no special equipment or environment. They are accessible wherever you are, whenever you need them.

Physical Activity

As discussed in the previous section, physical activity is not only crucial for physical health but also for mental well-being. Regular movement helps to dissipate the accumulation of stress hormones in the body. Sarah found that a quick walk, particularly during her lunch break, helped reset her stress levels and improve her focus for the afternoon.

Communication and Boundaries

Effective communication is a less talked about but vital stress management tool. For Sarah, learning to communicate her needs clearly at work and at home helped reduce misunderstandings and set realistic expectations with her colleagues and family. Setting boundaries, such as 'no work emails after 7 PM', also allowed her designated time to unwind and engage fully with her personal life.

Connecting with Others

Human connection can be a powerful antidote to stress. Conversations with friends or loved ones not only provide emotional support but can also help put your problems in perspective. Sarah made it a point to have coffee with a close friend once a week, using this time to vent, laugh, and forget her stressors for a while. These connections remind us that we're not alone in our struggles.

Relaxing Hobbies

Engaging in activities that you find relaxing and that take your mind off stress is another effective strategy. This could be anything from reading, knitting, gardening, or even solving puzzles. Sarah found solace in painting, a hobby she revisited on weekend afternoons which allowed her creative expression and mental relaxation.

Adequate Sleep

Never underestimate the power of sleep in combating stress. Lack of sleep can exacerbate stress by impairing cognitive function and emotional resilience. Sarah addressed her sleep hygiene by establishing a calm bedtime routine and sticking to a consistent schedule, even on weekends.

Nutrition

What we eat also plays a crucial role in how we cope with stress. A balanced diet rich in vegetables, fruits, lean proteins, and whole grains provides the necessary nutrients to fuel the brain and stabilize mood. While Sarah was no nutritional expert, making small, consistent changes such as reducing caffeine and sugar intake made noticeable differences in her stress levels.

Professional Help

Lastly, sometimes the best way to manage stress is by seeking professional help. Psychologists or counselors can provide strategies and tools uniquely tailored to your personal circumstances. For Sarah, a few sessions with a counselor helped her develop more robust coping mechanisms and regain her strength.

By integrating these practices into her daily routine, Sarah found that she was not only managing her stress better but was also enjoying her life more fully. Her journey is a testament to the fact that while stress may be inevitable, it doesn't have to dictate our lives. We can reclaim our tranquility and forge a path to a healthier, more balanced existence. Each of these strategies doesn't stand alone but intertwines with others, creating a comprehensive approach to stress management and self-care. Remember, taking time for stress management isn't a luxury—it's an essential part of maintaining your health and happiness.

5.3 Tracking Progress and Staying Motivated

Embarking on a journey to embed healthy habits into your daily routine can feel energizing and daunting in equal measure. The initial surge of motivation when you start out is exhilarating, yet maintaining that momentum can sometimes feel like pushing a boulder uphill. Let's delve into the stories and strategies that can help you track your progress and stay motivated, ensuring that your healthy intentions turn into enduring actions.

Consider the journey of Jack, a freelance graphic designer who decided to lead a healthier lifestyle. He was enthusiastic at the start—packing salads for lunch, taking brisk walks, sleeping earlier. However, as the novelty wore off, so did his motivation. What he found helpful was setting up a system to monitor his behaviors and celebrating small wins, which kept his spirits high and his goals in sight.

The Importance of Visible Progress

Visual reminders of your progress can serve as powerful motivators. For Jack, this meant creating a simple wall chart where he could tick off his daily goals. Each tick was a pat on the back, a tangible sign of his commitment. Alternatively, digital tracking tools or apps that log your meals, physical activity, and sleep can also serve this purpose. Seeing a visual representation of your week or month—understanding where you succeeded and where you faced challenges—provides invaluable insights into your habits and health.

Setting Achievable Goals

The key to sustainable motivation lies partly in setting goals that are realistic and achievable. If you aim too high too soon, you're more likely to feel discouraged. Break your primary goals into smaller, manageable tasks. For Jack, instead of vowing to "exercise every day," he started by incorporating three workout sessions a week into his routine. As he grew more comfortable, he gradually increased his activity. This method of scaling up ensured he could stay consistent without feeling overwhelmed.

Celebrating Milestones

It's crucial to recognize and celebrate milestones, no matter how small. These celebrations reinforce the positive behavior you're trying to cultivate. Jack had a small notebook where he would jot down each time he met a weekly goal and would treat himself to a movie or a small outing every time he filled a page. This not only created excitement around achieving his goals but also integrated fun rewards that kept the pursuit enjoyable.

The Power of Community

Sharing your progress with a supportive community can also amplify your motivation. Jack joined an online community of freelance professionals committed to health and wellness. Here, members shared their successes and setbacks, learning from each other. The encouragement and camaraderie found in such groups can be especially motivating on days when your personal enthusiasm wanes.

Reflective Journals

Keeping a reflective journal is another tool that helped Jack stay on track. He would spend a few minutes each evening reflecting on what went well and what could be improved. This practice not only ensured that he remained mindful of his daily behaviors but also helped him understand his motivations, challenges, and what truly helped him feel good both physically and emotionally.

Flexibility and Adaptability

Jack learned that rigidity in his routines often led to frustration during unexpected life events. Incorporating flexibility into his goals allowed him to adapt without feeling like he failed. When a project deadline demanded more hours, he adjusted his exercise from a gym session to a shorter home workout. Understanding and planning for such adjustments kept him from being overly critical of himself and helped maintain his overall motivation.

Regularly Reassess Goals

Over time, what we need from our routines can change, and so can our capabilities. Regularly reassessing and adjusting your goals is essential. Every month, Jack reviews his progress, celebrates his success, and sets new goals for the coming month. This not only revives his motivation but also aligns his activities with his evolving personal and professional life.

By emulating Jack's approach to integrating and maintaining healthy habits, you can create a self-reinforcing cycle of achievement and motivation. Tracking your progress, setting achievable goals, and incorporating flexibility are not just strategies but also acts of self-care. They signal to yourself that you are worth the effort. It is these daily affirmations, these consistent steps, that pave the path to lasting wellness and a vibrant, fulfilling life. Remember, every small step is a piece of the puzzle in your journey towards a healthier, happier you.

CHAPTER 6: DELICIOUS ZERO POINT BREAKFAST RECIPES

Imagine the sun peeking through your curtains, casting a golden glow over your morning—a new day brimming with possibilities and, of course, the need for a nourishing start. Breakfast, rightly dubbed as the most important meal of the day, sets the tone for the energy and focus levels we carry through the hustle of our schedules. But the truth is, amid our packed routines, whipping up a healthy and inspiring breakfast can sometimes feel like a tall order. This is exactly why Chapter 6: Delicious Zero Point Breakfast Recipes isn't just a collection of recipes—it's your new morning companion designed to transform your start-of-the-day ritual.

Each recipe curated in this chapter has been crafted keeping in mind those ticking clocks and your need for something quick yet supremely nutritious. These meals aren't just meals; they are vibrant, flavorful, and packed with ingredients that align perfectly with your zero point goals—meaning you can indulge without the guilt. We're talking about fluffy omelets, zesty smoothies, and hearty oats, each dish as satisfying and delightful as they are beneficial.

It's common to feel skeptical about the phrase 'quick and healthy.' How often have we encountered promises of convenience only to be met with bland flavors or unsatisfying portions? This chapter dispels those doubts by bringing you flavors from around the world, tailored to energize and satisfy, without any compromise. Think of these recipes as a tool—a way to reclaim your mornings, not just to eat but truly enjoy food that fuels your body and delights your palate.

With these recipes, you'll find more than just food; you'll discover mornings punctuated with moments of peace, a chance to savor your day's first flavors amidst the dawn's quiet. As you turn each page, look forward to seamless preparation methods that cater to your fast-paced life, allowing you to greet the day not just on-time but on a positive and healthful note.

Welcome to a sunrise like no other, filled with dishes that ensure each breakfast is an opportunity—not a chore—but a delightful, empowering way to start your day. Here's to beginning as we mean to go on, energized, satisfied, and ready to seize all our moments.

6.1 ENERGIZING MORNING SMOOTHIES

GREEN DETOX SMOOTHIE WITH SPINACH AND APPLE

Preparation Time: 5 min
Cooking Time: none

Mode of Cooking: Blending
Servings: 2 Serv.
Ingredients:
- 1 cup fresh spinach
- 1 large green apple, cored and chopped
- 1/2 banana
- 1/2 cup cucumber slices
- 1 Tbsp chia seeds
- 1 cup cold water
- 1/2 Tbsp fresh lemon juice

Directions:
1. Instructions: Combine spinach, green apple, banana, cucumber, chia seeds, and water in a blender.
2. Blend until smooth.

3. Add lemon juice and pulse to mix thoroughly.
4. Serve immediately in chilled glasses.

Additional Tips:

• Additional For an extra chill, you can add a few ice cubes before blending.

• If the smoothie is too thick, adjust the consistency by adding a little more water.

• Enhance sweetness naturally with a bit more banana if desired.

Nutritional Values: Calories: 95 kcal, Protein: 2g, Fat: 1g, Saturated Fat: 0g, Carbohydrates: 21g, Sugars: 13g, Fiber: 4g, Sodium: 16mg

SmartPoints Calculation: 4.3

BERRY BLAST SMOOTHIE WITH ALMOND MILK

Preparation Time: 5 min
Cooking Time: none
Mode of Cooking: Blending
Servings: 2
Ingredients:

• 1 cup mixed berries (strawberries, blueberries, raspberries)
• 1 cup unsweetened almond milk
• 1/2 banana
• 1 Tbsp ground flaxseed
• 1 tsp honey (optional)

Directions:

1. Instructions: Combine all berries, almond milk, banana, and flaxseed in a blender.
2. Blend until smooth.
3. Sweeten with honey if desired and blend again to mix.
4. Serve immediately.

Additional Tips:

• Additional Use frozen berries for a thicker texture and a cold smoothie without adding ice.

• Flaxseed adds omega-3 fatty acids but can be substituted with hemp seeds for a different nutrient profile.

Nutritional Values: Calories: 120 kcal, Protein: 2g, Fat: 3g, Saturated Fat: 0g, Carbohydrates: 22g, Sugars: 12g, Fiber: 5g, Sodium: 80mg

SmartPoints Calculation: 4.9

TROPICAL MANGO AND PINEAPPLE SMOOTHIE

Preparation Time: 5 min
Cooking Time: none
Mode of Cooking: Blending
Servings: 2
Ingredients:

• 1 cup mango, cubed
• 1/2 cup pineapple, cubed
• 1 banana
• 1 cup coconut water
• 1 Tbsp shredded coconut
• 1 tsp lime juice

Directions:

1. Instructions: Combine mango, pineapple, banana, and coconut water in a blender.
2. Blend until smooth.
3. Add shredded coconut and lime juice, then blend briefly to mix through.
4. Serve chilled.

Additional Tips:

• Additional For added protein, include a scoop of plain or vanilla protein powder.

• If you prefer a sweeter taste, consider adding a small amount of agave syrup.

• Garnish with a slice of lime or mint for an aesthetically pleasing presentation.

Nutritional Values: Calories: 140 kcal, Protein: 1g, Fat: 1g, Saturated Fat: 0.5g, Carbohydrates: 33g, Sugars: 25g, Fiber: 3g, Sodium: 42mg

SmartPoints Calculation: 7.3

CREAMY AVOCADO AND KALE SMOOTHIE

Preparation Time: 5 min
Cooking Time: none
Mode of Cooking: Blending
Servings: 2
Ingredients:

• 1/2 avocado
• 1 cup kale, stems removed
• 1/2 green apple, cored and chopped
• 1/2 banana

- 1 cup almond milk
- 1 Tbsp lemon juice
- 1 tsp ginger, grated

Directions:

1. Instructions: Combine avocado, kale, green apple, banana, and almond milk in a blender.
2. Blend until smooth.
3. Add lemon juice and ginger, blend until all ingredients are well integrated.
4. Serve immediately, garnished with a slice of avocado or a sprinkle of chia seeds.

Additional Tips:

- Additional If the smoothie is too thick, add more almond milk for a lighter consistency.
- Ginger not only adds a zesty flavor but also promotes digestion.
- For extra creaminess, you might add a spoonful of Greek yogurt.

Nutritional Values: Calories: 165 kcal, Protein: 3g, Fat: 9g, Saturated Fat: 1g, Carbohydrates: 20g, Sugars: 10g, Fiber: 5g, Sodium: 40mg
SmartPoints Calculation: 6.2

SUNRISE CITRUS ZINGER

Preparation Time: 5 min.
Cooking Time: none
Mode of Cooking: Blending
Servings: 2
Ingredients:

- 1 medium pink grapefruit, peeled and seeded
- 2 medium oranges, peeled and seeded
- 1/2 medium lemon, peeled and seeded
- 1/2 inch ginger root, peeled
- 1/4 tsp turmeric powder
- 1/2 cup ice cubes
- 1 Tbsp chia seeds

Directions:

1. Peel and section citrus fruits carefully to avoid including any pits and maximize pulp retention.
2. Place the prepared grapefruit, oranges, lemon, and ginger into the blender.
3. Add turmeric and ice cubes, then blend on high until the mixture reaches a smooth consistency.
4. Stir in chia seeds by hand after blending to retain their crunch and nutritional value.

Additional Tips:

- Adjust Citrus Levels: If the flavor is too tart, increase the proportion of orange or add a small spoonful of honey or agave syrup to adjust sweetness.
- Ginger Turmeric Balance: Start with smaller amounts of ginger and turmeric, then increase according to taste, as both can be quite potent.

Nutritional Values: Calories: 140 kcal, Protein: 2g, Fat: 1g, Saturated Fat: 0g, Carbohydrates: 34g, Sugars: 22g, Fiber: 6g, Sodium: 5mg
SmartPoints Calculation: 6.7

GREEN GINGER PEACH DELIGHT

Preparation Time: 6 min.
Cooking Time: none
Mode of Cooking: Blending
Servings: 2
Ingredients:

- 2 large peaches, pitted and sliced
- 1 cup unsweetened almond milk
- 1 handful baby spinach
- 1/2 inch piece of fresh ginger, peeled
- 1 Tbsp flax seeds
- 3-4 fresh mint leaves
- 1/2 cup ice cubes

Directions:

1. Combine peaches, almond milk, spinach, ginger, and ice cubes in a blender.
2. Blend until smooth, ensuring all ingredients are fully incorporated.
3. Once smooth, add flax seeds and blend for an additional 30 seconds to mix them thoroughly but maintain some texture.

Additional Tips:

- Mint Enhancement: Toss mint leaves in at the end of blending for a refreshing twist.

- Cooler Version: Use frozen peaches to make the smoothie colder and thicker, reducing the need for ice cubes.

Nutritional Values: Calories: 120 kcal, Protein: 3g, Fat: 3g, Saturated Fat: 0g, Carbohydrates: 24g, Sugars: 16g, Fiber: 5g, Sodium: 95mg

SmartPoints Calculation: 5.3

BERRY BEET BLISS

Preparation Time: 7 min.
Cooking Time: none
Mode of Cooking: Blending
Servings: 2
Ingredients:
- 1 medium beet, peeled and diced
- 1 cup mixed berries (strawberries, blueberries, raspberries)
- 1 cup coconut water
- 1 tsp lemon juice
- 1/2 cup plain non-fat Greek yogurt
- 1 Tbsp honey (optional)
- 1/2 cup ice cubes

Directions:
1. Place all ingredients except honey into a blender, starting with coconut water to facilitate smoother blending.
2. Blend on high until completely smooth.
3. Taste and blend in honey if a sweeter smoothie is desired.

Additional Tips:
- Extra Creaminess: Add more Greek yogurt for a creamier texture without significantly increasing calories.
- Berry Varieties: Experiment with different berry combinations each time to enjoy various flavors and benefits.

Nutritional Values: Calories: 130 kcal, Protein: 6g, Fat: 0.5g, Saturated Fat: 0g, Carbohydrates: 28g, Sugars: 20g (includes optional honey), Fiber: 4g, Sodium: 70mg

SmartPoints Calculation: 5.8

CUCUMBER MINT REFRESHER

Preparation Time: 5 min.
Cooking Time: none
Mode of Cooking: Blending
Servings: 2
Ingredients:
- 1 large cucumber, peeled and sliced
- 1/2 cup water
- 1/4 cup fresh lime juice
- 10 fresh mint leaves
- 1 tsp grated ginger
- 1/2 cup ice cubes
- 1 Tbsp honey (optional)

Directions:
1. Slice cucumber and gather all ingredients.
2. Place cucumber, water, lime juice, mint leaves, ginger, and ice in a blender.
3. Blend until smooth.
4. Add honey if a sweeter taste is preferred and blend again briefly.

Additional Tips:
- Cucumber Prep: Chill the cucumber before blending for a more refreshing drink.
- Lime Twist: Increase or decrease lime juice based on how tart you like your smoothies.
- Mint Modulation: Use fewer or more mint leaves based on your preference for mint flavor intensity.

Nutritional Values: Calories: 80 kcal, Protein: 1g, Fat: 0.5g, Saturated Fat: 0g, Carbohydrates: 19g, Sugars: 14g, Fiber: 2g, Sodium: 10mg

SmartPoints Calculation: 4

SUNRISE CITRUS ZINGER SMOOTHIE

Preparation Time: 5 mins
Cooking Time: none
Mode of Cooking: Blending
Servings: 2
Ingredients:
- 1 large ruby red grapefruit, peeled and deseeded
- 1 naval orange, peeled and deseeded
- 1/2 lemon, peeled and deseeded
- 1/2 cup carrot juice

- 1/2 inch fresh ginger, peeled
- 6 ice cubes

Directions:

1. Combine all ingredients in a high-powered blender.
2. Blend on high until completely smooth and frothy.
3. Pour into two glasses and serve immediately.

Additional Tips:

- Ginger Substitute: If fresh ginger is too strong, use a pinch of dried ginger powder for a milder taste.
- Make-Ahead Tip: Prepare portions of pre-peeled citrus in airtight containers for a quicker morning setup.
- Ice Cube Enhancement: For an extra flavor boost, freeze carrot juice in your ice cube trays and use these instead of plain ice cubes.

Nutritional Values: Calories: 120 kcal, Protein: 2g, Fat: 0.5g, Saturated Fat: 0g, Carbohydrates: 25g, Sugars: 18g, Fiber: 4g, Sodium: 60mg

SmartPoints Calculation: 5.6

GREEN TEA MINT MEDLEY SMOOTHIE

Preparation Time: 5 mins
Cooking Time: none
Mode of Cooking: Blending
Servings: 2
Ingredients:

- 2 cups chilled brewed green tea
- 1 cup fresh spinach leaves
- 1 large cucumber, peeled and sliced
- 1/2 apple, core removed, chopped
- 10 mint leaves
- Juice of 1 lime
- 1 Tbsp honey (optional)
- 8 ice cubes

Directions:

1. Place all ingredients into a blender.
2. Blend until smooth.
3. Pour into glasses and garnish with a sprig of mint, if desired.

Additional Tips:

- Cucumber Cooling Tip: For an extra cool drink, chill the cucumber in the refrigerator before blending.
- Sweetness Adjustment: Adjust the sweetness by adding or omitting honey based on personal preference.
- Lime Zest Garnish: Add a zest of lime on top of each smoothie for added aroma and flavor.

Nutritional Values: Calories: 70 kcal, Protein: 1g, Fat: 0g, Saturated Fat: 0g, Carbohydrates: 17g, Sugars: 13g, Fiber: 2g, Sodium: 20mg

SmartPoints Calculation: 3.6

6.2 HEARTY AND HEALTHY BREAKFAST BOWLS

QUINOA AND BERRY BREAKFAST BOWL

Preparation Time: 10 min
Cooking Time: 20 min
Mode of Cooking: Boiling
Servings: 4
Ingredients:

- 1 cup quinoa
- 2 cups water
- 1/2 tsp salt
- 1 cup fresh strawberries, sliced
- 1/2 cup blueberries
- 1/2 cup raspberries
- 1/4 cup sliced almonds
- 2 Tbsp honey
- 1 tsp cinnamon powder

Directions:

1. Rinse quinoa under cold water until water runs clear to remove the natural bitter coating.
2. In a medium saucepan, combine quinoa, water, and salt; bring to a boil over medium-high heat.
3. Reduce heat to low, cover, and simmer for 15 min. or until water is absorbed.
4. Remove from heat; let stand covered for 5 min. Fluff quinoa with a fork.

5. In serving bowls, divide the cooked quinoa. Top each with equal amounts of strawberries, blueberries, raspberries, and almonds.
6. Drizzle honey over each serving and sprinkle with cinnamon.

Additional Tips:
- Consider replacing honey with agave syrup for a lower glycemic index option.
- You can toast the almonds in a dry skillet for a nuttier flavor before adding them to the bowl.
- For added protein, a scoop of protein powder can be mixed into the quinoa after it is cooked and before adding the toppings.
- This bowl is equally delicious when served chilled, making it a great prepare-ahead breakfast option.

Nutritional Values: Calories: 290 kcal, Protein: 8g, Fat: 9g, Saturated Fat: 1g, Carbohydrates: 48g, Sugars: 12g, Fiber: 7g, Sodium: 300mg
SmartPoints Calculation: 9.8

CHIA SEED PUDDING WITH FRESH BERRIES

Preparation Time: 15 min
Cooking Time: none
Mode of Cooking: No Cooking
Servings: 4
Ingredients:
- 1/4 cup chia seeds
- 1 cup non-fat milk or almond milk
- 1/2 tsp vanilla extract
- 1 Tbsp honey
- 1 cup mixed berries (strawberries, blueberries, blackberries)

Directions:
1. In a bowl, mix chia seeds, milk, vanilla extract, and honey until well combined.
2. Cover the mixture and refrigerate overnight to allow the chia seeds to absorb the liquid and form a pudding-like consistency.
3. Before serving, stir the pudding again and adjust sweetness if needed.
4. Serve in individual bowls topped with a generous amount of mixed berries.

Additional Tips:
- Variety in your choice of berries can enhance the visual appeal and nutritional value.
- Almond milk can be substituted with coconut milk for a tropical twist.
- For added crunch, sprinkle granola on top before serving.
- If you find the pudding too thick, adjust its consistency by adding a bit more milk when serving.

Nutritional Values: Calories: 130 kcal, Protein: 4g, Fat: 5g, Saturated Fat: 0.5g, Carbohydrates: 18g, Sugars: 10g, Fiber: 7g, Sodium: 50mg
SmartPoints Calculation: 4.9

ZESTY TOFU AND SPINACH SCRAMBLE BOWL

Preparation Time: 15 mins
Cooking Time: 10 mins
Mode of Cooking: Sautéing
Servings: 2
Ingredients:
- 14 oz firm tofu, drained and crumbled
- 2 cups fresh spinach
- 1/4 cup diced red bell pepper
- 1 small red onion, finely chopped
- 2 cloves garlic, minced
- 1 tsp turmeric
- 1/2 tsp black salt (Kala Namak)
- 1 Tbsp nutritional yeast
- 1 Tbsp olive oil
- Salt and pepper to taste

Directions:
1. Heat olive oil in a non-stick skillet over medium heat.
2. Add chopped red onion and minced garlic, sauté until translucent.
3. Stir in red bell pepper and crumbled tofu, cook for about 5 mins, stirring frequently.
4. Sprinkle turmeric, black salt, and nutritional yeast; mix well to combine all ingredients.
5. Add fresh spinach, cook until wilted.
6. Season with salt and pepper to taste, remove from heat.
7. Serve warm in breakfast bowls.

Additional Tips:
- Try adding a splash of lemon juice for extra zest.
- Black salt adds a unique eggy flavor, making it perfect for vegan scrambles.
- Serve with a slice of whole-grain toast for a more filling meal.

Nutritional Values: Calories: 190 kcal, Protein: 18g, Fat: 10g, Saturated Fat: 1.5g, Carbohydrates: 9g, Sugars: 3g, Fiber: 4g, Sodium: 340mg
SmartPoints Calculation: 4.8

SMOKED SALMON AND AVOCADO BOWL

Preparation Time: 10 mins
Cooking Time: none
Mode of Cooking: No Cooking
Servings: 2
Ingredients:
- 4 oz smoked salmon
- 1 ripe avocado, peeled and sliced
- 1 cup arugula
- 1/2 cucumber, thinly sliced
- 1 Tbsp capers
- 2 tsp lemon juice
- 1 Tbsp chopped dill
- Salt and pepper to taste

Directions:
1. Arrange arugula at the bottom of the bowl.
2. Layer with thinly sliced cucumber and slices of avocado.
3. Top with smoked salmon and sprinkle capers and chopped dill over it.
4. Drizzle with lemon juice and season with salt and pepper to taste.
5. Serve chilled and fresh.

Additional Tips:
- Use wild-caught salmon for better flavor and nutritional benefits.
- The avocado provides healthy fats that keep you full for longer periods.
- For a dairy touch, add a dollop of non-fat Greek yogurt on the side.

Nutritional Values: Calories: 290 kcal, Protein: 23g, Fat: 20g, Saturated Fat: 3g, Carbohydrates: 9g, Sugars: 2g, Fiber: 7g, Sodium: 870mg
SmartPoints Calculation: 7.7

SUNNY MEDITERRANEAN BREAKFAST BOWL

Preparation Time: 20 mins
Cooking Time: 5 mins
Mode of Cooking: Sautéing
Servings: 2
Ingredients:
- 1 cup chopped kale
- 6 cherry tomatoes, halved
- 1/2 cup chickpeas, rinsed and drained
- 1 small zucchini, sliced
- 1/4 cup crumbled feta cheese
- 2 tsp olive oil
- 1 tsp smoked paprika
- Salt and pepper to taste
- 2 eggs

Directions:
1. Heat olive oil in a skillet over medium heat.
2. Sauté zucchini slices until golden, about 3 mins.
3. Add chickpeas and cherry tomatoes, cook for 2 more mins.
4. Stir in chopped kale, smoked paprika, salt, and pepper; cook until kale is slightly wilted.
5. In another pan, fry eggs to your liking.
6. Assemble bowls by dividing vegetable mix and placing a fried egg on top.
7. Sprinkle crumbled feta over the bowls.

Additional Tips:
- Swap feta cheese for non-fat Greek yogurt if desired for a creamier texture.
- Smoked paprika imparts a warm, smoky flavor that pairs well with the freshness of the vegetables.
- Serve with a whole-wheat pita for added fiber.

Nutritional Values: Calories: 250 kcal, Protein: 14g, Fat: 16g, Saturated Fat: 5g, Carbohydrates: 16g, Sugars: 4g, Fiber: 5g, Sodium: 580mg
SmartPoints Calculation: 8.1

Berry Almond Breakfast Quinoa

Preparation Time: 15 mins
Cooking Time: 20 mins
Mode of Cooking: Simmering
Servings: 2
Ingredients:
- 1 cup quinoa
- 2 cups water
- 1 cup mixed berries (fresh or frozen)
- 1/4 cup slivered almonds
- 1/4 tsp cinnamon
- 1 Tbsp honey
- 1 tsp vanilla extract

Directions:
1. Rinse quinoa under cold running water.
2. In a pot, combine quinoa and water, bring to a boil.
3. Reduce heat to low, cover, and simmer for 15 mins or until water is absorbed.
4. Remove from heat, let it sit covered for 5 mins.
5. Fluff quinoa with a fork, stir in vanilla extract, cinnamon, and honey.
6. Fold in mixed berries and slivered almonds.
7. Serve warm in bowls, drizzle extra honey if desired.

Additional Tips:
- Experiment with different types of berries to vary the flavor and color.
- Toasting the almonds before adding them to the bowl enhances their nutty flavor.
- For added protein, mix in a scoop of non-fat Greek yogurt.

Nutritional Values: Calories: 310 kcal, Protein: 8g, Fat: 8g, Saturated Fat: 0.5g, Carbohydrates: 50g, Sugars: 10g, Fiber: 7g, Sodium: 15mg
SmartPoints Calculation: 10

Greek Yogurt and Fruit Parfait Bowl

Preparation Time: 10 min
Cooking Time: none
Mode of Cooking: No Cooking
Servings: 4
Ingredients:
- 2 cups non-fat Greek yogurt
- 1/2 cup granola
- 1 banana, sliced
- 1/2 cup sliced strawberries
- 1/2 cup blueberries
- 1 Tbsp honey

Directions:
1. Layer half of the Greek yogurt at the bottom of four bowls.
2. Sprinkle each with granola, followed by a layer of banana slices.
3. Add the remaining yogurt then top with strawberries and blueberries.
4. Drizzle honey over each parfait.

Additional Tips:
- Substitute granola with nuts for a higher protein content.
- Experiment with different fruits like mango or kiwi to vary the flavor profile.
- Chilling the bowls before assembling the parfaits can add a refreshing touch to your breakfast.
- Layering the ingredients in a clear bowl or glass can make this simple breakfast look visually stunning.

Nutritional Values: Calories: 220 kcal, Protein: 14g, Fat: 3g, Saturated Fat: 0g, Carbohydrates: 36g, Sugars: 24g, Fiber: 3g, Sodium: 55mg
SmartPoints Calculation: 8.2

Oatmeal with Cinnamon and Sliced Apples

Preparation Time: 5 min
Cooking Time: 15 min
Mode of Cooking: Boiling
Servings: 4
Ingredients:
- 1 cup steel-cut oats
- 2 cups water
- 1 apple, peeled and thinly sliced
- 1 tsp cinnamon powder
- 1 Tbsp brown sugar

- 1/2 cup fat-free milk

Directions:

1. In a medium saucepan, bring water to a boil. Add oats and reduce heat to a simmer.
2. Cook, stirring occasionally, for about 15 min. or until oats are tender.
3. Remove from heat and stir in milk to achieve a creamy texture.
4. Serve the oatmeal in bowls topped with sliced apple, a sprinkle of cinnamon, and a dusting of brown sugar.

Additional Tips:

- Consider adding a pinch of nutmeg for added warmth and spice.
- Pre-cooking apples in a dash of cinnamon and a small amount of water can soften them and enhance the flavor integration.
- For those watching their sugar intake, substitute brown sugar with a sugar alternative.
- To keep it even healthier, opt for water instead of milk when cooking the oats.

Nutritional Values: Calories: 150 kcal, Protein: 5g, Fat: 2.5g, Saturated Fat: 0.5g, Carbohydrates: 27g, Sugars: 6g, Fiber: 4g, Sodium: 10mg

SmartPoints Calculation: 4.9

SUNRISE SALMON AND AVOCADO BOWL

Preparation Time: 15 min
Cooking Time: 10 min
Mode of Cooking: Grilling
Servings: 2
Ingredients:

- 1/2 lb fresh salmon fillet
- 1 ripe avocado, diced
- 2 cups baby spinach
- 1 small red onion, thinly sliced
- 1 Tbsp olive oil
- 1 tsp lemon zest
- 2 Tbsp lemon juice
- Salt and pepper to taste
- 1 Tbsp fresh dill, chopped

Directions:

1. Season the salmon: Brush the salmon fillet with 1/2 Tbsp olive oil, sprinkle with salt, pepper, and lemon zest.
2. Grill the salmon: Preheat the grill to medium-high heat (around 375°F or 190°C). Place the salmon skin side down, grilling for about 5 min on each side or until fully cooked and flakes easily.
3. Prepare the vegetables: In a bowl, toss baby spinach and red onion with the remaining olive oil and lemon juice.
4. Assemble the bowl: Arrange the spinach and onion mixture in bowls. Top with grilled salmon, diced avocado, and sprinkle with fresh dill.

Additional Tips:

- Swap avocado for cucumber for a crunchier texture.
- Lemon zest enhances the fresh flavor, but lime zest can be used for a tropical twist.
- Serve immediately to enjoy the full flavor of the grilled salmon.

Nutritional Values: Calories: 290 kcal, Protein: 23g, Fat: 17g, Saturated Fat: 3g, Carbohydrates: 9g, Sugars: 2g, Fiber: 4g, Sodium: 70mg

SmartPoints Calculation: 7.7

MUSHROOM AND SPINACH FRITTATA CUPS

Preparation Time: 20 min
Cooking Time: 25 min
Mode of Cooking: Baking
Servings: 6
Ingredients:

- 6 eggs
- 1 cup diced mushrooms
- 2 cups spinach, roughly chopped
- 1/4 cup non-fat milk
- 1/2 tsp salt
- 1/4 tsp pepper
- 1/4 cup reduced-fat feta cheese, crumbled
- 1 tsp olive oil
- 1/2 tsp garlic powder

Directions:

1. Whisk together eggs and milk: In a large bowl, combine eggs, non-fat milk, salt, pepper, and garlic powder, beating until well mixed.
2. Sauté vegetables: Heat olive oil in a skillet over medium heat, add mushrooms, and sauté for 3 min. Add spinach and cook until wilted. Remove from heat and let cool slightly.
3. Combine and fill: Stir sautéed vegetables and feta cheese into the egg mixture. Pour evenly into greased muffin tins, filling each cup about three-quarters full.
4. Bake the frittata cups: Preheat the oven to 350°F (175°C). Bake for 20-25 min or until the tops are firm to the touch and eggs are cooked.

Additional Tips:

- Use silicone muffin cups for easy release of the frittatas without the need for greasing.
- Add a sprinkle of paprika or chili flakes for an extra kick.
- Pair with a side of zero-point salsa for added flavor without additional points.

Nutritional Values: Calories: 100 kcal, Protein: 9g, Fat: 6g, Saturated Fat: 2g, Carbohydrates: 2g, Sugars: 1g, Fiber: 0g, Sodium: 220mg
SmartPoints Calculation: 2.8

6.3 QUICK AND EASY BREAKFAST OPTIONS

OVERNIGHT OATS WITH ALMOND BUTTER AND BANANA

Preparation Time: 10 min
Cooking Time: none
Mode of Cooking: No Cooking
Servings: 2
Ingredients:

- 1 cup rolled oats
- 1.5 cups unsweetened almond milk
- 2 Tbsp almond butter
- 1 medium banana, sliced
- 1 Tbsp chia seeds
- 1 tsp vanilla extract
- 1 Tbsp honey (optional)
- Pinch of salt

Directions:

1. Combine Ingredients: In a medium-sized bowl, mix rolled oats, unsweetened almond milk, chia seeds, vanilla extract, and a pinch of salt.
2. Layer and Chill: Spoon half of the mixture into two jars, add a layer of almond butter and a layer of sliced banana. Top with the remaining oat mixture. Close the jars and refrigerate overnight.
3. Serve: The next morning, stir the oats well. If desired, drizzle with honey and add extra slices of banana before serving.

Additional Tips:

- Mason Jars for Portability: Use mason jars for assembling the oats for an easy, portable breakfast option.
- Customize with Nuts: Add chopped almonds or walnuts for extra crunch and protein.
- Increase Sweetness Naturally: Enhance sweetness with more banana or a drizzle of honey if avoiding refined sugars.

Nutritional Values: Calories: 345 kcal, Protein: 10g, Fat: 14g, Saturated Fat: 1.5g, Carbohydrates: 50g, Sugars: 12g, Fiber: 9g, Sodium: 180mg
SmartPoints Calculation: 11.4

VEGGIE-PACKED EGG MUFFINS

Preparation Time: 15 min
Cooking Time: 20 min
Mode of Cooking: Baking
Servings: 6
Ingredients:

- 6 large eggs
- 1 cup chopped spinach
- 1/2 cup diced red bell pepper
- 1/4 cup diced onions
- 1/2 cup crumbled feta cheese
- 1/4 tsp salt
- 1/4 tsp black pepper

Directions:
1. Prepare: Preheat oven to 375°F (190°C). Grease a 6-cup muffin pan or use silicone muffin liners.
2. Mix Eggs: In a large bowl, whisk eggs together with salt and black pepper.
3. Add Vegetables and Cheese: Stir in chopped spinach, diced red bell pepper, diced onions, and crumbled feta cheese.
4. Bake: Divide the mixture evenly among the muffin cups. Bake for 20 min or until the muffins are set and lightly golden on top.
5. Serve: Let cool for a few minutes before removing from the muffin pan. Serve warm.

Additional Tips:
- Easy Meal Prep: Make a batch at the start of the week for an easy grab-and-go breakfast option.
- Veggie Variations: Experiment with different vegetables like mushrooms or zucchini for variety.
- Cheese Options: Swap feta cheese for another low-fat cheese like mozzarella if preferred.

Nutritional Values: Calories: 140 kcal, Protein: 10g, Fat: 10g, Saturated Fat: 4g, Carbohydrates: 3g, Sugars: 2g, Fiber: 1g, Sodium: 340mg
SmartPoints Calculation: 4.6

WHOLE GRAIN TOAST WITH AVOCADO AND TOMATO

Preparation Time: 5 min
Cooking Time: none
Mode of Cooking: No Cooking
Servings: 1
Ingredients:
- 1 slice whole grain bread, toasted
- 1/2 ripe avocado, mashed
- 1 small tomato, sliced
- A sprinkle of sea salt
- A sprinkle of crushed red pepper flakes
- 1 tsp olive oil

Directions:
1. Prepare Toast: Toast the slice of whole grain bread to your desired crispness.
2. Assemble: Spread the mashed avocado evenly over the toasted bread. Layer with sliced tomato.
3. Season and Serve: Sprinkle with sea salt and crushed red pepper flakes. Drizzle with olive oil and serve immediately.

Additional Tips:
- Quick Customization: Add a poached egg on top for extra protein.
- Extra Flavor: Garnish with fresh basil or cilantro for an herby touch.
- Avocado Ripeness: Use a perfectly ripe avocado for the best creaminess and flavor.

Nutritional Values: Calories: 250 kcal, Protein: 6g, Fat: 18g, Saturated Fat: 3g, Carbohydrates: 20g, Sugars: 3g, Fiber: 7g, Sodium: 300mg
SmartPoints Calculation: 8.2

COTTAGE CHEESE WITH PINEAPPLE CHUNKS

Preparation Time: 5 min
Cooking Time: none
Mode of Cooking: No Cooking
Servings: 1
Ingredients:
- 1 cup low-fat cottage cheese
- 1/2 cup pineapple chunks, fresh or canned (in juice, drained)
- 1 Tbsp shredded coconut, unsweetened
- 1 Tbsp chopped nuts (optional)

Directions:
1. Mix: In a bowl, combine low-fat cottage cheese with pineapple chunks.
2. Add Toppings: Sprinkle with unsweetened shredded coconut and chopped nuts if using.
3. Serve: Enjoy this sweet and refreshing breakfast that is also packed with protein.

Additional Tips:
- Protein Boost: Add a scoop of your favorite protein powder to the cottage cheese for an extra protein kick.
- Tropical Twist: Mix in other tropical fruits like mango or papaya for variety.

- Nut Choices: Use almonds, walnuts, or pecans for added texture and healthy fats.

Nutritional Values: Calories: 220 kcal, Protein: 20g, Fat: 8g, Saturated Fat: 4g, Carbohydrates: 18g, Sugars: 15g, Fiber: 1g, Sodium: 500mg

SmartPoints Calculation: 7.7

ZESTY GINGER-PEACH YOGURT PARFAIT

Preparation Time: 15 min
Cooking Time: none
Mode of Cooking: No Cooking
Servings: 2
Ingredients:
- 2 large fresh peaches, peeled and diced
- 1 cup non-fat Greek yogurt
- 1 tsp fresh ginger, grated
- 2 Tbsp honey
- 1/4 cup granola
- A pinch of nutmeg

Directions:
1. Combine the Greek yogurt with grated fresh ginger and honey in a mixing bowl.
2. Place half of the diced peaches at the bottom of two serving glasses.
3. Layer each glass with half of the yogurt mixture.
4. Add the remaining peaches on top of the yogurt layer in each glass.
5. Sprinkle granola and a pinch of nutmeg on top of the peaches.
6. Chill in the refrigerator until ready to serve.

Additional Tips:
- Serve Chilled: For a refreshing start to your morning, ensure that the parfait is chilled at least for an hour before serving.
- Fresh Peach Alternative: If fresh peaches are not available, thawed frozen peaches can be a convenient substitute.
- Nut-Free Option: Omit granola or use a nut-free alternative to accommodate allergies.

Nutritional Values: Calories: 150 kcal, Protein: 8g, Fat: 2g, Saturated Fat: 0.5g, Carbohydrates: 28g, Sugars: 20g, Fiber: 2g, Sodium: 50mg

SmartPoints Calculation: 6.3

SAVORY SPINACH AND MUSHROOM EGG WHITE CUPS

Preparation Time: 20 min
Cooking Time: 25 min
Mode of Cooking: Baking
Servings: 6
Ingredients:
- 1 cup fresh spinach, chopped
- 1/2 cup mushrooms, finely chopped
- 1/4 cup red bell pepper, diced
- 6 egg whites
- 1/4 cup skim milk
- Salt and pepper to taste
- Cooking spray

Directions:
1. Preheat the oven to 375°F (190°C).
2. Lightly spray a 6-cup muffin tin with cooking spray.
3. In a bowl, whisk together egg whites, skim milk, salt, and pepper.
4. Stir in the spinach, mushrooms, and red bell pepper.
5. Pour the egg mixture evenly into the muffin cups.
6. Bake in the preheated oven until the egg whites are set, about 25 min.
7. Let cool for 5 min before serving.

Additional Tips:
- Batch Cooking: Prepare multiple batches and store in the refrigerator for a quick on-the-go breakfast during the week.
- Veggie Variations: Mix in other vegetables like onions, tomatoes, or zucchini for added flavor and nutrition.
- Dairy-Free Version: Replace skim milk with almond milk for a dairy-free alternative.

Nutritional Values: Calories: 70 kcal, Protein: 8g, Fat: 0.5g, Saturated Fat: 0g, Carbohydrates: 3g, Sugars: 2g, Fiber: 1g, Sodium: 170mg

SmartPoints Calculation: 1.6

WARM CINNAMON APPLE QUINOA BOWL

Preparation Time: 10 min
Cooking Time: 20 min
Mode of Cooking: Simmering
Servings: 2
Ingredients:
- 1 apple, diced
- 1/2 cup quinoa, rinsed
- 1 cup water
- 1/2 tsp cinnamon
- 1 Tbsp chopped walnuts
- 2 tsp honey

Directions:
1. Combine water, quinoa, and cinnamon in a small saucepan and bring to a boil.
2. Reduce heat to low, cover, and simmer until quinoa is cooked, about 20 min.
3. Stir in diced apple and allow to sit, covered, for 5 min.
4. Transfer to bowls and top with chopped walnuts and drizzle with honey.

Additional Tips:
- Quinoa Prep Rinse quinoa thoroughly under cold water to remove its natural coating, which can be bitter.
- Apple Selection: Use a sweet variety like Fuji or Honeycrisp for natural sweetness.
- Add-In Variety: Incorporate dried fruits or a spoonful of nut butter for extra flavor and richness.

Nutritional Values: Calories: 235 kcal, Protein: 6g, Fat: 5g, Saturated Fat: 0.5g, Carbohydrates: 42g, Sugars: 12g, Fiber: 5g, Sodium: 10mg
SmartPoints Calculation: 8.2

SPICY TOMATO AND WHITE BEAN TOAST

Preparation Time: 15 min
Cooking Time: 5 min
Mode of Cooking: Toasting
Servings: 2
Ingredients:
- 2 slices whole grain bread
- 1/2 cup white beans, cooked and drained
- 1 small tomato, diced
- 1/2 small red onion, finely chopped
- 1 Tbsp olive oil
- 1/2 tsp crushed red pepper flakes
- Salt and pepper to taste
- Fresh basil leaves for garnish

Directions:
1. Toast whole grain bread slices to your preference.
2. In a bowl, combine white beans, diced tomato, chopped red onion, olive oil, and red pepper flakes. Season with salt and pepper.
3. Spoon the bean mixture over the toasted bread slices.
4. Garnish with fresh basil leaves before serving.

Additional Tips:
- Bean Mix Advance Prep: Prepare the bean mixture in advance and store in the refrigerator to allow flavors to meld.
- Tomato Tip: For added flavor, use heirloom tomatoes when available.
- Spice Adjustment: Reduce or increase red pepper flakes based on your preferred spice level.

Nutritional Values: Calories: 200 kcal, Protein: 9g, Fat: 7g, Saturated Fat: 1g, Carbohydrates: 29g, Sugars: 4g, Fiber: 6g, Sodium: 200mg
SmartPoints Calculation: 6

SUNRISE SMOOTHIE BOWL

Preparation Time: 7 min
Cooking Time: none
Mode of Cooking: Blending
Servings: 1
Ingredients:
- 1 cup frozen mixed berries
- 1/2 ripe banana
- 1/2 cup non-fat Greek yogurt
- 1/4 cup unsweetened almond milk
- 1 Tbsp chia seeds
- 1/4 tsp pure vanilla extract
- 1 Tbsp unsweetened shredded coconut
- 1 Tbsp sliced almonds
- 1/2 Tbsp raw honey (optional)

Directions:

1. Combine berries, banana, Greek yogurt, almond milk, chia seeds, and vanilla extract in a high-powered blender.
2. Blend until smooth and thick.
3. Pour the mixture into a bowl and garnish with shredded coconut, sliced almonds, and drizzle with honey if using.
4. Serve immediately and enjoy your vibrant, energy-boosting breakfast.

Additional Tips:

- Use frozen fruit for a thicker consistency: Choosing frozen berries gives the bowl a creamy, ice-cream-like texture without needing ice.
- Add more nuts for extra crunch: Feel free to substitute sliced almonds with other nuts like walnuts or pecans for varied textures and flavors.
- Sweetening alternatives: If avoiding honey, consider a splash of stevia or agave syrup for a lower-calorie sweetness.

Nutritional Values: Calories: 285 kcal, Protein: 14g, Fat: 9g, Saturated Fat: 1g, Carbohydrates: 40g, Sugars: 20g, Fiber: 9g, Sodium: 110mg
SmartPoints Calculation: 10

PEPPERED MUSHROOM & SPINACH OMELET

Preparation Time: 10 min
Cooking Time: 8 min
Mode of Cooking: Sautéing, Simmering
Servings: 2
Ingredients:

- 3 egg whites
- 1 whole egg
- 1/2 cup chopped spinach
- 1/2 cup sliced mushrooms
- 1/4 tsp cracked black pepper
- 1/4 tsp sea salt
- 1 tsp olive oil
- 2 Tbsp crumbled feta cheese
- 2 Tbsp chopped green onions

Directions:

1. Heat olive oil in a non-stick skillet over medium heat.
2. Sauté mushrooms until they're golden and soft.
3. Add spinach and cook until wilted.
4. In a bowl, whisk together egg whites, whole egg, salt, and pepper.
5. Pour egg mixture into the skillet over the sautéed vegetables.
6. Cook for about 3-4 min until the edges start to lift from the pan. Flip and cook the other side for 1-2 min.
7. Sprinkle with feta cheese and green onions before serving.

Additional Tips:

- Experiment with vegetables: Swap spinach and mushrooms for bell peppers and onions for a different flavor profile.
- Lower-fat protein options: Substitute feta cheese with a lower-fat cheese like ricotta or cottage cheese if preferred.
- Serving suggestion: Serve with a side of roasted tomatoes for added flavor and freshness.

Nutritional Values: Calories: 175 kcal, Protein: 18g, Fat: 9g, Saturated Fat: 3g, Carbohydrates: 4g, Sugars: 2g, Fiber: 1g, Sodium: 510mg
SmartPoints Calculation: 4.6

CHAPTER 7: SATISFYING ZERO POINT LUNCH RECIPES

Imagine this: it's midday, your morning rush has just tapered off, and your stomach begins its familiar rumble. Lunchtime approaches, but so does the challenge—how do you quell your hunger without derailing your wellness goals? This is where the beauty of Zero Point Lunch Recipes comes into play, crafting the perfect midday meal that satisfies without compromise.

In Chapter 7, we dive into the heart of day-to-day wellness with lunch recipes that are as fulfilling as they are nutritious. These aren't just meals; they are your secret weapon in achieving and sustaining your weight loss without feeling deprived or succumbing to the midday slump. The recipes you'll discover here are crafted with the busy professional in mind—easy to prepare, portable if needed, and diverse to cater to a variety of tastes and dietary needs.

Think of a lunch that recharges your energy without leaving you feeling sluggish as you head back to your desk or resume your daily tasks. We explore vibrant salads that leap far beyond the typical lettuce and tomato fare, brimming with flavors that span the globe—from the zesty zest of a Thai mango salad to the robust earthiness of a Tuscan white bean salad. And for those colder days, imagine cozying up to a bowl of aromatic soup that warms your body and lifts your spirits, all while aligning with your wellness objectives.

Each recipe in this chapter aligns with the Zero Point philosophy, which prioritizes high nutrient density with low calorie impact, allowing you to eat satisfying portions without tipping the scales. Moreover, these lunch ideas are designed to keep you full longer, helping curb those afternoon cravings that too often lead to unwise snacking.

As you turn the pages of this chapter, envision yourself not just eating, but thoroughly enjoying meals that fuel your body and support your wellness journey—one delicious bite at a time. This isn't just about maintaining a diet; it's about enriching a lifestyle. So, let's set the table for a lunchtime revolution that keeps you energized, satisfied, and on track with your health goals.

7.1 FRESH AND FLAVORFUL SALADS

GRILLED PEACH AND CHICKEN SALAD

Preparation Time: 15 min
Cooking Time: 10 min
Mode of Cooking: Grilling
Servings: 4

Ingredients:
- 2 large peaches, halved and pitted
- 2 boneless, skinless chicken breasts
- 1 Tbsp olive oil
- Salt and pepper to taste
- 4 cups arugula
- 1/2 red onion, thinly sliced
- 1/4 cup crumbled feta cheese
- 2 Tbsp balsamic glaze

Directions:

1. Brush peaches and chicken breasts with olive oil and season with salt and pepper.
2. Preheat grill to medium-high heat (approximately 375°F or 190°C). Grill chicken breasts for 5-6 min per side or until fully cooked. Grill peaches cut side down, until charred, about 4-5 min.

3. Slice grilled chicken and peaches.
4. In a large salad bowl, toss arugula and red onion. Top with sliced chicken, grilled peaches, and crumbled feta. Drizzle balsamic glaze over the salad.
5. Serve immediately for a delightful mix of sweet, savory, and tangy flavors.

Additional Tips:
- Use a grill pan if outdoor grilling isn't an option - it works just as well for peaches and chicken.
- If balsamic glaze is too strong, dilute with a bit of olive oil for a milder dressing.
- Arugula can be substituted with mixed greens for a less peppery flavor.

Nutritional Values: Calories: 290 kcal, Protein: 26g, Fat: 12g, Saturated Fat: 3g, Carbohydrates: 20g, Sugars: 15g, Fiber: 3g, Sodium: 320mg
SmartPoints Calculation: 8.9

ZESTY LIME SHRIMP AND AVOCADO SALAD

Preparation Time: 20 min
Cooking Time: none
Mode of Cooking: No Cooking
Servings: 4
Ingredients:
- 400g raw shrimp, peeled and deveined
- 2 avocados, diced
- 1 large cucumber, diced
- 1/4 cup chopped red onion
- 2 Tbsp chopped cilantro
- Juice of 2 limes
- Salt and pepper to taste

Directions:
1. Marinate shrimp in lime juice, salt, and pepper for 10 min.
2. In a large bowl, combine diced avocado, cucumber, red onion, and cilantro.
3. Add marinated shrimp to the avocado mixture. Toss gently to mix.
4. Serve chilled, garnished with additional cilantro if desired. This salad is refreshing with a zesty lime kick ideal for a light lunch.

Additional Tips:
- Add a pinch of chili flakes to the shrimp marinade for extra spice.
- This salad can also be served as a filling in low-carb wraps for a quick meal on the go.
- To prevent avocado from browning, toss the diced pieces in a little extra lime juice.

Nutritional Values: Calories: 215 kcal, Protein: 15g, Fat: 15g, Saturated Fat: 2g, Carbohydrates: 10g, Sugars: 2g, Fiber: 7g, Sodium: 180mg
SmartPoints Calculation: 5.9

CRISPY TOFU AND KALE SALAD WITH TAHINI DRESSING

Preparation Time: 15 min
Cooking Time: 20 min
Mode of Cooking: Baking
Servings: 4
Ingredients:
- 400g firm tofu, pressed and cubed
- 2 Tbsp soy sauce
- 2 Tbsp olive oil
- 1 tsp garlic powder
- 4 cups chopped kale
- 1 carrot, shredded
- 1/4 cup tahini
- 2 Tbsp lemon juice
- 2 tsp maple syrup
- Salt and pepper to taste

Directions:
1. Marinate tofu cubes in soy sauce, olive oil, and garlic powder for 15 min.
2. Preheat oven to 400°F (200°C). Spread tofu on a baking sheet and bake for 20 min, turning halfway through, until crisp.
3. Whisk together tahini, lemon juice, maple syrup, salt, and pepper to make the dressing.
4. In a large bowl, toss kale and carrot. Add baked tofu and drizzle with tahini dressing. Toss again to coat evenly.
5. Serve this hearty salad warm or at room temperature.

Additional Tips:

- For extra crunch, add toasted sesame seeds to the salad before serving.
- Kale can be massaged with a little olive oil prior to adding other ingredients to soften its texture.
- If maple syrup is unavailable, honey can be used as a sweetener substitute in the dressing.

Nutritional Values: Calories: 330 kcal, Protein: 18g, Fat: 25g, Saturated Fat: 3g, Carbohydrates: 15g, Sugars: 3g, Fiber: 4g, Sodium: 530mg
SmartPoints Calculation: 9.5

BEETROOT AND GOAT CHEESE SALAD WITH WALNUTS

Preparation Time: 15 min
Cooking Time: none
Mode of Cooking: No Cooking
Servings: 4
Ingredients:

- 4 medium beets, cooked, peeled, and sliced
- 100g goat cheese, crumbled
- 1/2 cup walnuts, toasted and chopped
- 2 Tbsp olive oil
- 1 Tbsp red wine vinegar
- Salt and pepper to taste
- Mixed salad greens (optional)

Directions:

1. In a large salad bowl, arrange sliced beets and sprinkle with crumbled goat cheese and walnuts.
2. Whisk together olive oil, red wine vinegar, salt, and pepper to create the dressing.
3. Pour dressing over the beetroot, cheese, and walnuts. Toss gently to combine.
4. Serve on a bed of mixed salad greens for extra freshness.

Additional Tips:

- Experiment with different types of beets like golden or candy-striped for a visually appealing dish.
- Goat cheese can be replaced with feta for a sharper taste.
- Add a handful of fresh herbs like parsley or basil to enhance the flavors.

Nutritional Values: Calories: 290 kcal, Protein: 10g, Fat: 22g, Saturated Fat: 5g, Carbohydrates: 15g, Sugars: 10g, Fiber: 4g, Sodium: 360mg
SmartPoints Calculation: 10.4

TANGY CITRUS FENNEL SALAD

Preparation Time: 15 mins
Cooking Time: none
Mode of Cooking: No Cooking
Servings: 4
Ingredients:

- 2 large fennel bulbs
- 3 oranges, peeled and segmented
- 1 small red onion, thinly sliced
- a handful of arugula leaves
- 2 Tbsp fresh lemon juice
- 1 Tbsp extra virgin olive oil
- 1 tsp honey
- Sea salt and black pepper to taste

Directions:

1. Prepare the Ingredients: Start by thinly slicing the fennel bulbs and red onion, and segmenting the oranges.
2. Combine Salad: In a large bowl, toss together fennel, oranges, red onion, and arugula.
3. Dress the Salad: Whisk together lemon juice, olive oil, honey, sea salt, and black pepper. Drizzle over the salad and toss gently to coat everything evenly.
4. Chill and Serve: Let the salad chill in the refrigerator for about 10 minutes before serving to merge the flavors together.

Additional Tips:

- Use Blood Oranges for Extra Color and Flavor: The deep red of blood oranges adds a stunning contrast to the pale fennel and can be a visually striking addition.
- Salad Spinner for Fennel: After slicing, use a salad spinner to remove any excess moisture from the fennel so the salad remains crisp and not soggy.

- Serving Suggestion: Serve this salad as a refreshing start to a summer meal or alongside grilled fish for a light dinner.

Nutritional Values: Calories: 140 kcal, Protein: 2g, Fat: 5g, Saturated Fat: 0.7g, Carbohydrates: 22g, Sugars: 15g, Fiber: 6g, Sodium: 85mg

SmartPoints Calculation: 6.1

ASIAN SLAW WITH PEANUT DRESSING

Preparation Time: 20 mins
Cooking Time: none
Mode of Cooking: No Cooking
Servings: 4
Ingredients:
- 4 cups shredded Napa cabbage
- 1 cup shredded carrots
- 1 red bell pepper, thinly sliced
- 1/4 cup chopped fresh cilantro
- 1/4 cup sliced green onions
- 2 Tbsp crushed peanuts
- For the dressing: 2 Tbsp peanut butter
- 1 Tbsp soy sauce
- 1 Tbsp rice vinegar
- 2 tsp sesame oil
- 1 tsp honey
- 1 clove garlic, minced
- 1 tsp grated fresh ginger

Directions:
1. Prepare the Vegetables: Shred cabbage, carrots, and slice the red bell pepper and green onions.
2. Make the Dressing: In a small bowl, combine peanut butter, soy sauce, rice vinegar, sesame oil, honey, minced garlic, and grated ginger. Whisk until smooth and consistent.
3. Combine Salad and Dressing: In a large bowl, toss together the cabbage, carrots, bell pepper, cilantro, and green onions. Pour the dressing over and toss well to coat.
4. Garnish and Serve: Sprinkle the crushed peanuts over the top just before serving.

.Additional Tips:
- Dressing Consistency Adjustment: If the dressing is too thick, add a few teaspoons of warm water to thin it out to the desired consistency.
- Colorful Slaw Variations: Add purple cabbage for an additional vibrant color and nutritional boost.
- Lighten It Up: For an even lower-calorie version, use powdered peanut butter mixed with water in place of regular peanut butter.

Nutritional Values: Calories: 180 kcal, Protein: 6g, Fat: 11g, Saturated Fat: 2g, Carbohydrates: 14g, Sugars: 8g, Fiber: 4g, Sodium: 240mg

SmartPoints Calculation: 6.4

MEDITERRANEAN CHICKPEA SALAD

Preparation Time: 10 mins
Cooking Time: none
Mode of Cooking: No Cooking
Servings: 6
Ingredients:
- 2 cans (15 oz each) of chickpeas, rinsed and drained
- 1 cucumber, diced
- 2 plum tomatoes, diced
- 1/4 cup chopped kalamata olives
- 1/4 cup feta cheese, crumbled
- 1/4 cup red onion, finely chopped
- 2 Tbsp chopped fresh parsley
- For the dressing: 3 Tbsp extra virgin olive oil
- 1 Tbsp lemon juice
- 1 tsp dried oregano
- Salt and pepper to taste

Directions:
1. Combine Salad Ingredients: In a large bowl, mix chickpeas, cucumber, tomatoes, kalamata olives, crumbled feta, red onion, and parsley.
2. Whisk Together Dressing: In a small bowl, whisk together olive oil, lemon juice, oregano, salt, and pepper.
3. Dress the Salad: Pour the dressing over the salad ingredients and toss well to coat.
4. Chill Before Serving: Allow the salad to chill in the refrigerator for at least 30 minutes to let the flavors meld together.

Additional Tips:
- Add a Protein Boost: Toss in some grilled chicken or tofu to add a protein punch for a more filling meal.
- Make Ahead: This salad can be prepared a day in advance, making it perfect for busy schedules and ensuring even more flavorful results as the ingredients mingle.
- Dietary Adjustments: For a vegan version, omit the feta cheese or replace it with a vegan alternative.

Nutritional Values: Calories: 230 kcal, Protein: 8g, Fat: 10g, Saturated Fat: 2g, Carbohydrates: 29g, Sugars: 5g, Fiber: 8g, Sodium: 400mg
SmartPoints Calculation: 7.4

SPICY WATERMELON AND CUCUMBER GAZPACHO

Preparation Time: 15 mins
Cooking Time: none
Mode of Cooking: No Cooking
Servings: 4
Ingredients:
- 4 cups cubed seedless watermelon
- 1 large cucumber, peeled and chopped
- 1 small jalapeño, seeded and minced
- 1/4 cup red onion, minced
- 1/4 cup fresh mint leaves
- 2 Tbsp lime juice
- 1 Tbsp extra virgin olive oil
- Salt to taste

Directions:
1. Prepare Ingredients: Chop watermelon, cucumber, and mince jalapeño and red onion.
2. Blend the Gazpacho: Place the watermelon, cucumber, jalapeño, red onion, mint leaves, lime juice, and olive oil in a blender. Blend until smooth.
3. Chill: Transfer the gazpacho to a container and refrigerate for at least 2 hours to cool.
4. Serve Chilled: Stir the gazpacho well before serving. Season with salt to taste and garnish with additional mint if desired.

Additional Tips:
- Spice Level Adjustment: Adjust the number of jalapeños according to your spice preference. Remove seeds to reduce heat if necessary.
- Serving Suggestion: Serve this refreshing soup on hot summer days as a light appetizer or a palate cleanser between courses.
- Garnish Options: Garnish with diced avocado or a scoop of non-fat Greek yogurt for a creamy texture and added flavors.

Nutritional Values: Calories: 120 kcal, Protein: 2g, Fat: 5g, Saturated Fat: 0.5g, Carbohydrates: 18g, Sugars: 12g, Fiber: 2g, Sodium: 10mg
SmartPoints Calculation: 5

ROASTED BEET AND GOAT CHEESE SALAD

Preparation Time: 10 min
Cooking Time: 45 min
Mode of Cooking: Roasting
Servings: 4
Ingredients:
- 4 medium beets, scrubbed
- 1/3 cup crumbled goat cheese
- 1/4 cup chopped walnuts, toasted
- 2 Tbsp balsamic vinegar
- 1 Tbsp honey
- 3 Tbsp extra-virgin olive oil
- Salt and pepper to taste
- Mixed greens for serving

Directions:
1. Roast Beets: Preheat oven to 375°F (190°C). Wrap beets in foil and place on a baking sheet. Roast until tender, about 45 min.
2. Cool and Peel: Allow beets to cool, then peel and dice.
3. Prepare Dressing: In a small bowl, whisk together balsamic vinegar, honey, olive oil, salt, and pepper.
4. Combine Ingredients: In a salad bowl, mix the roasted beets, goat cheese, and toasted walnuts. Pour over the dressing and toss gently.
5. Serve: Place the beet mixture over a bed of mixed greens and serve immediately.

Additional Tips:
- Beet Prep Shortcut: Use pre-cooked and peeled beets to save on prep time.
- Alternate Cheese Options: Feta or bleu cheese can be used in place of goat cheese for a different flavor.
- Additional Flavor: Add a sprinkle of orange zest or a few slices of fresh orange to the salad for a fresh, citrusy lift.

Nutritional Values: Calories: 275 kcal, Protein: 7g, Fat: 21g, Saturated Fat: 5g, Carbohydrates: 17g, Sugars: 13g, Fiber: 4g, Sodium: 200mg

SmartPoints Calculation: 10.6

ASIAN SESAME EDAMAME SALAD

Preparation Time: 10 min
Cooking Time: none
Mode of Cooking: No Cooking
Servings: 4
Ingredients:
- 2 cups shelled edamame, cooked and cooled
- 1 red bell pepper, thinly sliced
- 1 cup shredded purple cabbage
- 1/2 cup thinly sliced green onions
- 1/4 cup sesame seeds, toasted
- 3 Tbsp sesame oil
- 2 Tbsp soy sauce
- 1 Tbsp rice vinegar
- 1 clove garlic, minced
- 1 inch piece of ginger, grated
- 1 tablespoon honey
- Salt and pepper to taste

Directions:
1. Combine Ingredients: In a large bowl mix edamame, red bell pepper, purple cabbage, green onions, and half of the sesame seeds.
2. Mix Dressing: In a small bowl, whisk together sesame oil, soy sauce, rice vinegar, minced garlic, grated ginger, honey, salt, and pepper until well blended.
3. Dress and Toss: Pour the dressing over the vegetable mixture and toss to coat thoroughly.
4. Garnish and Serve: Sprinkle with remaining sesame seeds and serve chilled or at room temperature.

Additional Tips:
- Swap Soy Sauce: Use tamari or coconut aminos for a gluten-free alternative.
- Enhance Sweetness: Add a touch of fresh orange juice to the dressing for a slight sweet twist.ия
- Serving Suggestion: Serve this salad as a side with grilled fish or chicken for a complete meal.

Nutritional Values: Calories: 190 kcal, Protein: 12g, Fat: 12g, Saturated Fat: 2g, Carbohydrates: 13g, Sugars: 5g, Fiber: 5g, Sodium: 320mg

SmartPoints Calculation: 5.8

7.2 WHOLESOME SANDWICHES AND WRAPS

TURKEY AND AVOCADO LETTUCE WRAP

Preparation Time: 10 min
Cooking Time: none
Mode of Cooking: No Cooking
Servings: 2
Ingredients:
- 1/2 lb cooked turkey breast, shredded
- 1 ripe avocado, diced
- 1/2 cup cherry tomatoes, halved
- 1/4 red onion, finely sliced
- 4 large lettuce leaves, such as Romaine or Butter lettuce
- 1 Tbsp lime juice
- 1/4 tsp cumin
- Salt and pepper to taste

Directions:
1. Combine the turkey, avocado, cherry tomatoes, and red onion in a bowl.
2. Season with lime juice, cumin, salt, and pepper, and gently toss to mix.
3. Divide the mixture among the lettuce leaves, wrapping each leaf around the filling to form wraps.
4. Serve immediately for the freshest taste and best texture.

Additional Tips:
- Use iceberg lettuce for a crunchier texture.
- Pre-cook and refrigerate the turkey for a quicker assembly.
- For a zestier flavor, add a pinch of chili powder.
- To boost fiber, include a spoonful of cooked quinoa into the mix.

Nutritional Values: Calories: 290 kcal, Protein: 25g, Fat: 15g, Saturated Fat: 2.5g, Carbohydrates: 12g, Sugars: 2g, Fiber: 6g, Sodium: 70mg

SmartPoints Calculation: 7.3

GRILLED CHICKEN AND VEGGIE WRAP WITH HUMMUS

Preparation Time: 15 min
Cooking Time: 10 min
Mode of Cooking: Grilling
Servings: 4
Ingredients:
- 2 boneless, skinless chicken breasts
- 1 zucchini, sliced lengthwise
- 1 bell pepper, sliced
- 4 whole wheat wraps
- 1/2 cup hummus
- Baby spinach leaves
- 1 Tbsp olive oil
- Salt and pepper to taste

Directions:
1. Brush chicken breasts and sliced veggies with olive oil, season with salt and pepper, and grill over medium heat until the chicken is cooked and veggies are tender.
2. Slice the grilled chicken.
3. Spread hummus on each wrap, add a layer of baby spinach, then top with grilled chicken and veggies.
4. Roll up the wraps tightly, slice in half, and serve.

Additional Tips:
- Adapt the vegetables based on seasonality for fresher flavors.
- Add sliced avocados or a sprinkle of feta cheese for extra richness.
- Rolling the wraps tightly helps to keep the ingredients secure.

Nutritional Values: Calories: 350 kcal, Protein: 28g, Fat: 12g, Saturated Fat: 2g, Carbohydrates: 33g, Sugars: 3g, Fiber: 6g, Sodium: 400mg

SmartPoints Calculation: 8.8

TUNA SALAD LETTUCE WRAP WITH PICKLES

Preparation Time: 10 min
Cooking Time: none
Mode of Cooking: No Cooking
Servings: 2
Ingredients:
- 1 can (5 oz) tuna in water, drained
- 1/4 cup diced pickles
- 2 Tbsp non-fat Greek yogurt
- 1 Tbsp Dijon mustard
- 4 large lettuce leaves, such as Iceberg or Bibb
- 1/4 tsp paprika
- Salt and pepper to taste

Directions:
1. Mix tuna, diced pickles, Greek yogurt, and Dijon mustard in a bowl.
2. Season with paprika, salt, and pepper.
3. Spoon the tuna mixture into the lettuce leaves and wrap them to enclose the filling.
4. Serve chilled for a refreshing and light meal.

Additional Tips:
- Try adding capers for an extra tang.
- Use curried yogurt to introduce a warm spice flavor.
- Double up on lettuce leaves if they tear easily while wrapping.

Nutritional Values: Calories: 90 kcal, Protein: 15g, Fat: 1g, Saturated Fat: 0g, Carbohydrates: 3g, Sugars: 2g, Fiber: 1g, Sodium: 480mg

SmartPoints Calculation: 1.5

EGG SALAD SANDWICH WITH WHOLE GRAIN BREAD

Preparation Time: 15 min
Cooking Time: none
Mode of Cooking: No Cooking

Servings: 2
Ingredients:
- 4 hard-boiled eggs, chopped
- 2 Tbsp non-fat Greek yogurt
- 1 tsp mustard
- 4 slices whole grain bread
- Lettuce leaves
- 1/4 cup celery, finely diced
- 1/4 tsp smoked paprika
- Salt and pepper to taste

Directions:
1. Combine chopped eggs, Greek yogurt, mustard, and diced celery in a bowl.
2. Season with smoked paprika, salt, and pepper, and mix thoroughly.
3. Arrange lettuce leaves on two slices of bread, spread the egg mixture evenly, then top with the remaining bread slices.
4. Cut sandwiches in half and serve.

Additional Tips:
- Consider using avocado in place of some yogurt for creaminess.
- Add chopped herbs like dill or chives for a fresh burst.
- Lightly toasting the bread can add a nice crunch and flavor depth.

Nutritional Values: Calories: 310 kcal, Protein: 20g, Fat: 15g, Saturated Fat: 4g, Carbohydrates: 23g, Sugars: 5g, Fiber: 6g, Sodium: 620mg
SmartPoints Calculation: 9.2

ZESTY LEMON-PEPPER TOFU WRAP

Preparation Time: 15 min
Cooking Time: 10 min
Mode of Cooking: Sautéing
Servings: 4
Ingredients:
- 1 lb firm tofu, drained and pressed
- 2 Tbsp olive oil
- 1 large lemon, zested and juiced
- 1 tsp cracked black pepper
- 1/2 tsp sea salt
- 4 whole wheat tortillas
- 1 cup arugula
- 1/2 red onion, thinly sliced
- 1/2 cucumber, sliced
- 1/4 cup non-fat Greek yogurt

Directions:
1. Drain and press tofu to remove excess moisture, then slice into 1/2-inch thick strips.
2. In a bowl, whisk together lemon zest, lemon juice, olive oil, cracked black pepper, and sea salt. Add tofu strips and marinate for 10 minutes.
3. Heat a non-stick skillet over medium-high heat. Add tofu strips and sauté until golden on both sides, approximately 5 min per side.
4. Warm tortillas according to package instructions.
5. Lay out tortillas; spread a tablespoon of Greek yogurt on each. Top with arugula, cucumber slices, red onion, and sautéed tofu. Roll up tightly to form wraps.

Additional Tips:
- Use whole wheat or multigrain tortillas for extra fiber.
- Swap arugula for baby spinach for a milder taste.
- Add a drizzle of sriracha for a spicy kick.

Nutritional Values: Calories: 295 kcal, Protein: 18g, Fat: 15g, Saturated Fat: 2g, Carbohydrates: 28g, Sugars: 3g, Fiber: 6g, Sodium: 400mg
SmartPoints Calculation: 8.1

SMOKED SALMON AND CUCUMBER NORI ROLLS

Preparation Time: 20 min
Cooking Time: none
Mode of Cooking: No Cooking
Servings: 4
Ingredients:
- 4 nori seaweed sheets
- 8 oz smoked salmon
- 1 large cucumber, julienned
- 1 avocado, thinly sliced
- 1/4 cup non-fat Greek yogurt
- Wasabi paste to taste

- Soy sauce for dipping

Directions:
1. Lay out nori sheets on a flat surface.
2. Spread Greek yogurt thinly across each sheet.
3. Place slices of smoked salmon, julienned cucumber, and avocado near the bottom edge of each nori sheet.
4. Carefully roll the nori tightly from the bottom around the filling, using a sushi mat if available.
5. Slice each roll into six pieces. Serve with a small amount of soy sauce and wasabi paste.

Additional Tips:
- Nori is rich in minerals and creates a flavorful wrap without the carbs.
- Use a bamboo sushi mat for tighter rolls.
- Experiment with adding thinly sliced carrots or bell peppers for extra crunch and color.

Nutritional Values: Calories: 210 kcal, Protein: 17g, Fat: 12g, Saturated Fat: 2g, Carbohydrates: 6g, Sugars: 1g, Fiber: 4g, Sodium: 670mg
SmartPoints Calculation: 5.4

SPICY CHICKPEA AND SPINACH WRAP

Preparation Time: 15 min
Cooking Time: 20 min
Mode of Cooking: Baking
Servings: 4
Ingredients:
- 1 can (15 oz) chickpeas, drained and rinsed
- 1 Tbsp olive oil
- 1 tsp chili powder
- 1/2 tsp garlic powder
- 1/2 tsp onion powder
- 1/4 tsp sea salt
- 4 whole wheat wraps
- 2 cups fresh spinach
- 1/2 cup roasted red peppers, sliced
- 1/4 cup non-fat Greek yogurt

Directions:
1. Preheat oven to 400°F (200°C).
2. Toss chickpeas with olive oil, chili powder, garlic powder, onion powder, and sea salt until well-coated. Spread on a baking sheet.
3. Bake for 20 min until chickpeas are crispy.
4. Remove chickpeas from oven and let cool.
5. To assemble wraps, spread Greek yogurt on each wrap, then layer with fresh spinach, roasted red peppers, and crispy chickpeas. Roll up tightly to serve.

Additional Tips:
- Experiment with different spices like cumin or paprika for varied flavors.
- Add a squeeze of lemon or a few slices of avocado for extra zest and creaminess.

Nutritional Values: Calories: 290 kcal, Protein: 10g, Fat: 10g, Saturated Fat: 1g, Carbohydrates: 42g, Sugars: 5g, Fiber: 8g, Sodium: 470mg
SmartPoints Calculation: 8.7

GRILLED VEGETABLE AND GOAT CHEESE BURRITO

Preparation Time: 20 min
Cooking Time: 10 min
Mode of Cooking: Grilling
Servings: 4
Ingredients:
- 1 zucchini, sliced longitudinally
- 1 yellow bell pepper, seeded and quartered
- 1 red bell pepper, seeded and quartered
- 1 red onion, sliced into rings
- 2 Tbsp olive oil
- Sea salt to taste
- Cracked black pepper to taste
- 4 large whole wheat tortillas
- 1/4 cup goat cheese, crumbled
- 1/4 cup fresh basil leaves

Directions:
1. Preheat grill to medium-high heat.
2. Brush zucchini, bell peppers, and red onion with olive oil and season with salt and pepper.
3. Grill vegetables until tender and charred, about 5 min per side.
4. Once grilled, slice vegetables into strips.

5. Warm tortillas according to package instructions.
6. Divide grilled vegetables evenly among tortillas, top with crumbled goat cheese and fresh basil. Roll up and serve warm.

Additional Tips:
- Substitute goat cheese with feta for a tangier flavor.
- Add a splash of balsamic vinegar before rolling for a sweet acidity.
- Serve with a side of mixed greens for a complete meal.

Nutritional Values: Calories: 325 kcal, Protein: 11g, Fat: 17g, Saturated Fat: 5g, Carbohydrates: 35g, Sugars: 7g, Fiber: 6g, Sodium: 420mg
SmartPoints Calculation: 11

CHIMICHURRI CHICKPEA SALAD WRAP

Preparation Time: 15 mins
Cooking Time: none
Mode of Cooking: No Cooking
Servings: 4
Ingredients:
- 1 can chickpeas (15 oz, drained and rinsed)
- 1 cup fresh parsley, finely chopped
- 1/4 cup fresh cilantro, finely chopped
- 2 Tbsp red wine vinegar
- 3 Tbsp olive oil
- 1 clove garlic, minced
- 1 tsp dried oregano
- 1/2 tsp salt
- 1/4 tsp red pepper flakes
- 4 whole wheat tortillas
- 1 cup diced tomatoes
- 1/2 cup diced red bell peppers

Directions:
1. Mixing Salad: In a bowl, combine chickpeas, parsley, cilantro, red wine vinegar, olive oil, minced garlic, oregano, salt, and red pepper flakes. Stir well to coat all chickpeas.
2. Assembling Wraps: Spread each tortilla with the chickpea salad, top with diced tomatoes and red bell peppers.
3. Roll and Serve: Roll the tortillas tightly, slice in half, and serve immediately.

Additional Tips:
- Chill for Flavor: If time allows, let the chickpea mixture chill in the refrigerator for an hour to enhance the flavors.
- Wrap Stability: Wrap tightly and cut with a serrated knife to maintain the shape and ensure easy eating.

Nutritional Values: Calories: 310 kcal, Protein: 10g, Fat: 18g, Saturated Fat: 2.5g, Carbohydrates: 29g, Sugars: 5g, Fiber: 8g, Sodium: 320mg
SmartPoints Calculation: 9.8

SPICY GRILLED VEGGIE & HUMMUS WRAP

Preparation Time: 10 mins
Cooking Time: 10 mins
Mode of Cooking: Grilling
Servings: 4
Ingredients:
- 1 zucchini, sliced longitudinally
- 1 yellow squash, sliced longitudinally
- 1 medium red onion, sliced into rings
- 1 Tbsp olive oil
- 1 tsp smoked paprika
- 1/2 tsp chili powder
- 4 large whole wheat tortillas
- 1 cup homemade hummus
- 1 cup arugula

Directions:
1. Grilling Veggies: Toss zucchini, squash, and onion rings with olive oil, smoked paprika, and chili powder. Grill over medium heat until charred and tender, about 10 mins, turning occasionally.
2. Assembling Wraps: Spread each tortilla with hummus, lay grilled vegetables and arugula evenly among the tortillas.
3. Rolling and Serving: Roll up tortillas snugly, cut in half crosswise, and serve.

Additional Tips:
- Veggie Variety: Try different vegetables like bell peppers or eggplants for variation.

- Make Ahead: Prepare vegetables and hummus in advance to assemble wraps quickly at mealtime.
- Serving Suggestion: Serve with a side of light Greek yogurt for dipping.

Nutritional Values: Calories: 295 kcal, Protein: 11g, Fat: 14g, Saturated Fat: 2g, Carbohydrates: 35g, Sugars: 6g, Fiber: 8g, Sodium: 390mg

SmartPoints Calculation: 9.2

7.3 WARM AND COMFORTING SOUPS

CHICKEN AND VEGETABLE SOUP

Preparation Time: 20 min
Cooking Time: 40 min
Mode of Cooking: Simmering
Servings: 4
Ingredients:
- 2 skinless chicken breasts
- 3 large carrots, diced
- 1 large onion, chopped
- 2 stalks celery, diced
- 2 cloves garlic, minced
- 4 cups low-sodium chicken broth
- 1 tsp dried thyme
- 1 bay leaf
- Salt and pepper to taste
- 2 cups chopped spinach

Directions:
1. Instructions: Begin by heating a large soup pot over medium heat and adding the chicken breasts, onion, garlic, carrots, and celery.
2. Cook until the vegetables are softened and chicken is slightly browned, about 10 minutes.
3. Add the low-sodium chicken broth, dried thyme, bay leaf, and bring to a boil.
4. Reduce heat to a simmer, cover, and let cook for 30 minutes, or until the chicken is cooked through.
5. Remove the chicken from the pot, shred it, and return it to the soup.
6. Stir in the chopped spinach, season with salt and pepper, and cook for an additional 5 minutes.
7. Remove the bay leaf before serving.

Additional Tips:
- Additional To make this soup in a shorter time, use pre-cooked chicken and add it when you add the broth.
- Enhance flavor by sautéing the vegetables in 2 tsp of olive oil before adding the chicken.
- Serve with a dollop of non-fat Greek yogurt for an extra creamy texture.

Nutritional Values: Calories: 165 kcal, Protein: 25g, Fat: 2.5g, Saturated Fat: 0.5g, Carbohydrates: 13g, Sugars: 5g, Fiber: 3g, Sodium: 300mg

SmartPoints Calculation: 3.3

BUTTERNUT SQUASH AND CARROT SOUP

Preparation Time: 15 min
Cooking Time: 30 min
Mode of Cooking: Boiling
Servings: 4
Ingredients:
- 4 cups cubed butternut squash
- 3 large carrots, sliced
- 1 large onion, chopped
- 4 cups vegetable broth
- 1 clove garlic, minced
- 1 tsp ground cinnamon
- 1/4 tsp ground nutmeg
- Salt and pepper to taste
- Chopped parsley for garnish

Directions:
1. Instructions: Combine the butternut squash, carrots, onion, and garlic in a large pot.
2. Cover with vegetable broth and bring to a boil.
3. Reduce heat to low and simmer until vegetables are tender, about 20 minutes.
4. Use an immersion blender to puree the soup directly in the pot, or transfer to a blender in batches if necessary.
5. Stir in ground cinnamon, ground nutmeg, and season with salt and pepper.
6. Simmer for an additional 10 minutes.
7. Garnish with chopped parsley before serving.

Additional Tips:

- Additional For a smoother consistency, strain the soup through a fine mesh after blending.
- Add a splash of coconut milk for a creamier texture without adding too many calories.
- Serve this soup as a warm starter during chilly seasons.

Nutritional Values: Calories: 175 kcal, Protein: 3g, Fat: 0.5g, Saturated Fat: 0.1g, Carbohydrates: 41g, Sugars: 9g, Fiber: 7g, Sodium: 250mg

SmartPoints Calculation: 6.2

TOMATO BASIL SOUP WITH GRILLED SHRIMP

Preparation Time: 15 min
Cooking Time: 20 min
Mode of Cooking: Grilling and Simmering
Servings: 4
Ingredients:

- 4 cups chopped tomatoes
- 1/2 cup fresh basil, chopped
- 1 onion, chopped
- 2 cloves garlic, minced
- 3 cups low-sodium vegetable broth
- 12 large shrimp, peeled and deveined
- 1 tsp olive oil
- Salt and pepper to taste
- Basil leaves for garnish

Directions:

1. Instructions: Heat a grill to medium-high and brush the shrimp with olive oil, season with salt and pepper, and grill each side for about 2 minutes or until opaque.
2. In a soup pot, sauté onions and garlic until translucent.
3. Add chopped tomatoes, chopped basil, and vegetable broth. Bring to a boil, then reduce heat and simmer for 15 minutes.
4. Blend the soup using an immersion blender until smooth.
5. Serve the soup in bowls, topped with grilled shrimp and garnish with fresh basil leaves.

Additional Tips:

- Additional For extra flavor, add a pinch of red pepper flakes into the soup while it simmers.
- Marinate shrimp in a mixture of garlic, lemon juice, and herbs before grilling for enhanced flavor.
- Serve with a side of whole-grain toast for a complete meal.

Nutritional Values: Calories: 180 kcal, Protein: 18g, Fat: 3g, Saturated Fat: 0.5g, Carbohydrates: 22g, Sugars: 14g, Fiber: 5g, Sodium: 480mg

SmartPoints Calculation: 5.5

LENTIL AND SPINACH SOUP

Preparation Time: 10 min
Cooking Time: 45 min
Mode of Cooking: Boiling
Servings: 4
Ingredients:

- 1 cup dry lentils
- 3 cups fresh spinach
- 1 large carrot, diced
- 1 onion, diced
- 1 clove garlic, minced
- 4 cups low-sodium chicken broth
- 1 tsp cumin
- Salt and pepper to taste
- Lemon wedges for serving

Directions:

1. Instructions: Rinse lentils and set aside.
2. In a large pot, sauté onion, garlic, and carrots until onion is translucent.
3. Add the rinsed lentils and low-sodium chicken broth to the pot, bring to a boil.
4. Reduce heat to low, cover, and simmer until lentils are tender, about 35 minutes.
5. Stir in fresh spinach and cumin, cook until spinach is wilted, about 5 minutes.
6. Season with salt and pepper, and serve with lemon wedges.

Additional Tips:

- Additional For a richer flavor, sauté vegetables in 1 Tbsp of olive oil before adding lentils and broth.

- To add a tangy kick to the soup, squeeze a lemon wedge into each bowl before serving.
- This soup freezes well, so consider making a double batch and saving some for a busy day.

Nutritional Values: Calories: 230 kcal, Protein: 18g, Fat: 1g, Saturated Fat: 0g, Carbohydrates: 39g, Sugars: 4g, Fiber: 16g, Sodium: 300mg
SmartPoints Calculation: 5.7

SAFFRON INFUSED CAULIFLOWER SOUP

Preparation Time: 20 min
Cooking Time: 30 min
Mode of Cooking: Steaming and Blending
Servings: 4
Ingredients:
- 1 large cauliflower, cut into florets
- 1 large onion, finely chopped
- 2 cloves garlic, minced
- 4 cups vegetable broth
- 1 tsp turmeric
- 1 pinch saffron threads
- Salt and black pepper to taste
- 1 Tbsp chopped fresh parsley for garnish

Directions:
1. Wash and steam cauliflower florets until tender, approximately 15 min.
2. In a separate pan, sauté onion and garlic until translucent.
3. Add the steamed cauliflower, turmeric, saffron, and vegetable broth to the pan.
4. Simmer on medium heat for 15 min.
5. Blend the mixture until smooth using an immersion blender.
6. Season with salt and black pepper.
7. Serve hot, garnished with fresh parsley.

Additional Tips:
- Using a pinch of quality saffron provides a luxurious aroma and golden color.
- If you prefer a creamier texture, add a dollop of non-fat Greek yogurt before blending.
- Enhance the herbal note by garnishing with additional fresh herbs like chives or cilantro if parsley is not your preference.

Nutritional Values: Calories: 90 kcal, Protein: 4g, Fat: 3g, Saturated Fat: 0g, Carbohydrates: 15g, Sugars: 5g, Fiber: 6g, Sodium: 300mg
SmartPoints Calculation: 3

MISO MUSHROOM BROTH

Preparation Time: 15 min
Cooking Time: 25 min
Mode of Cooking: Simmering
Servings: 4
Ingredients:
- 4 cups low-sodium vegetable stock
- 1 cup shiitake mushrooms, thinly sliced
- 1 Tbsp miso paste
- 2 tsp ginger, grated
- 1 clove garlic, minced
- 2 Tbsp green onions, chopped
- 1 Tbsp low-sodium soy sauce
- 1 tsp sesame oil
- Tofu cubes, 100g

Directions:
1. Heat stock in a large pot over medium heat.
2. Add sliced mushrooms, ginger, and garlic; simmer for 20 min.
3. Remove from heat and stir in miso paste, soy sauce, sesame oil, and tofu cubes.
4. Serve hot topped with green onions.

Additional Tips:
- Do not boil the soup after adding miso to preserve its probiotic benefits.
- Stir miso with a small amount of broth before adding to avoid clumps.
- Enhance the umami flavor by adding a dash of dried seaweed during the cooking process.

Nutritional Values: Calories: 130 kcal, Protein: 8g, Fat: 5g, Saturated Fat: 1g, Carbohydrates: 15g, Sugars: 4g, Fiber: 3g, Sodium: 400mg
SmartPoints Calculation: 3.9

LEMON PEPPER VEGGIE SOUP

Preparation Time: 15 min
Cooking Time: 20 min
Mode of Cooking: Boiling

Servings: 4
Ingredients:
- 2 zucchinis, diced
- 1 yellow bell pepper, chopped
- 1 large carrot, diced
- 4 cups vegetable broth
- Juice and zest of 1 lemon
- 1 tsp cracked black pepper
- Salt to taste
- Fresh basil leaves, chopped for garnish

Directions:
1. Bring broth to a boil in a large pot.
2. Add zucchinis, bell pepper, and carrot; boil until vegetables are tender, about 15 min.
3. Add lemon juice, zest, and black pepper.
4. Simmer for an additional 5 min.
5. Season with salt.
6. Serve hot, garnished with fresh basil.

Additional Tips:
- Lemon zest adds a vibrant flavor, use organic lemons for the best taste.
- Use varying colors of bell peppers to make the dish visually appealing.
- For a protein boost, consider adding chickpeas in the last 5 min of boiling.

Nutritional Values: Calories: 80 kcal, Protein: 2g, Fat: 1g, Saturated Fat: 0g, Carbohydrates: 17g, Sugars: 8g, Fiber: 4g, Sodium: 250mg
SmartPoints Calculation: 3.2

SPICY TOMATO AND RED LENTIL SOUP

Preparation Time: 10 min
Cooking Time: 30 min
Mode of Cooking: Simmering
Servings: 4
Ingredients:
- 1 cup red lentils
- 4 cups vegetable broth
- 2 cups diced tomatoes
- 1 onion, finely chopped
- 2 cloves garlic, minced
- 1 Tbsp olive oil
- 1 tsp cumin
- 1 tsp chili flakes
- Salt and black pepper to taste
- Fresh coriander, chopped for garnish

Directions:
1. Heat oil in a pot and sauté onion and garlic until golden.
2. Add diced tomatoes, red lentils, cumin, chili flakes, and vegetable broth.
3. Bring to a boil then simmer on low heat until lentils are tender, about 25 min.
4. Blend slightly for a chunky texture.
5. Season with salt and pepper.
6. Serve hot, garnished with fresh coriander.

Additional Tips:
- Opt for low-acid tomatoes to prevent heartburn.
- Add a swirl of low-fat Greek yogurt for creaminess.
- If too spicy, adjust by reducing chili flakes and adding a bit more broth.

Nutritional Values: Calories: 180 kcal, Protein: 11g, Fat: 3g, Saturated Fat: 0g, Carbohydrates: 30g, Sugars: 6g, Fiber: 8g, Sodium: 200mg
SmartPoints Calculation: 5.1

MISO UMAMI SOUP

Preparation Time: 15 mins
Cooking Time: 20 mins
Mode of Cooking: Simmering
Servings: 4
Ingredients:
- 4 cups vegetable broth
- 2 Tbsp miso paste
- 1 cup cubed tofu
- 1 cup sliced shiitake mushrooms
- 1 large carrot, thinly sliced
- 2 green onions, chopped
- 1 tsp grated ginger
- 1 tsp soy sauce
- 1 tsp sesame oil
- 1 handful fresh spinach leaves

Directions:

1. Combine the vegetable broth, grated ginger, and soy sauce in a pot and bring to a simmer.
2. Dissolve the miso paste in a small amount of the warm broth before adding it back into the pot to avoid clumps.
3. Add the shiitake mushrooms and carrots to the broth and simmer until tender, about 10 mins.
4. Incorporate the cubed tofu and cook for an additional 5 mins.
5. Remove from heat and stir in the sesame oil, green onions, and fresh spinach just before serving.

Additional Tips:

- Use low-sodium soy sauce to keep the sodium content in check.
- Fresh ginger enhances flavor without adding calories.
- Serve hot with a sprinkle of toasted sesame seeds for extra crunch and flavor.

Nutritional Values: Calories: 90 kcal, Protein: 6g, Fat: 3g, Saturated Fat: 0.5g, Carbohydrates: 8g, Sugars: 3g, Fiber: 2g, Sodium: 450mg

SmartPoints Calculation: 2.7

CREAMY ROASTED CAULIFLOWER SOUP

Preparation Time: 10 mins
Cooking Time: 25 mins
Mode of Cooking: Roasting and Blending
Servings: 4
Ingredients:

- 1 head of cauliflower, cut into florets
- 3 cups vegetable broth
- 1 onion, chopped
- 2 cloves garlic, minced
- 2 Tbsp non-fat Greek yogurt
- 1 tsp olive oil
- 1/4 tsp nutmeg
- Salt and pepper to taste
- Chopped chives for garnish

Directions:

1. Roast the cauliflower florets with olive oil in a preheated oven at 425°F (220°C) for 20 mins until golden and tender.
2. Sauté onion and garlic in a pot with a splash of vegetable broth until translucent.
3. Add roasted cauliflower and remaining broth; simmer for 5 mins.
4. Blend the mixture until smooth, then stir in Greek yogurt and nutmeg. Reheat gently without boiling.
5. Serve garnished with chives.

Additional Tips:

- Opt for non-fat Greek yogurt to add creaminess without the extra fat.
- Roasting cauliflower brings out a nutty, sweet flavor that enhances the soup.
- Nutmeg adds a subtle warmth without overpowering the other flavors.

Nutritional Values: Calories: 110 kcal, Protein: 5g, Fat: 2g, Saturated Fat: 0.3g, Carbohydrates: 20g, Sugars: 6g, Fiber: 4g, Sodium: 300mg

SmartPoints Calculation: 3.7

CHAPTER 8: NOURISHING ZERO POINT DINNER RECIPES

As the sun dips below the horizon, casting a golden hue over your bustling kitchen, the evening meal often becomes more than just food—it becomes a moment of connection. With the demands of the day slowing to a gentle pause, dinner is when we gather, share and nourish not just our bodies but our spirits. In this chapter, we explore the art of creating enticing, zero-point dinners that promise flavor and fulfillment without burdening your calorie count.

Imagine walking through your door after a long day, your mind juggling deadlines and meetings, only to be greeted by the soothing aromas of a simmering pot on the stove. These are the evenings we yearn for, aren't they? Meals that offer comfort without the guilt, satisfaction without the struggle. The recipes you'll discover here are crafted keeping in mind that very essence—the fusion of simplicity and taste.

Dinners, I believe, should be a lighthouse guiding you safely home in the stormy sea of daily stresses and challenges. That's why the recipes in this section are designed to be straightforward and fuss-free, focusing on fresh ingredients and easy cooking methods. You will find dishes that are both a delight to prepare and a joy to serve. From savory stews that hug your soul to vibrant salads that refresh and revitalize, each recipe is a stepping stone towards maintaining a healthy weight and a happier you.

This chapter is not just about feeding the stomach but also about feeding the soul. It's about transforming a simple weeknight dinner into a nourishing ritual. Let these zero-point dinners reassure you that it's possible to indulge in delicious, hearty meals while on your journey to wellness. So, pull up a chair, take a deep breath, and prepare to turn the evening meal into a powerful tool in your wellness arsenal. Here, we redefine what it means to dine well, proving once and for all that health and happiness are found not in restriction, but in the wise embrace of all that nourishes us.

8.1 PROTEIN-PACKED MAIN DISHES

ZESTY LEMON DILL BAKED SALMON

Preparation Time: 15 min
Cooking Time: 20 min
Mode of Cooking: Baking
Servings: 4
Ingredients:

- 4 salmon fillets (6 oz each)
- Zest of 1 lemon
- 2 Tbsp fresh dill, chopped
- 1 Tbsp olive oil
- Juice of half a lemon
- Salt and pepper to taste

Directions:

1. Preheat oven to 375°F (190°C)
2. In a small bowl, mix lemon zest, chopped dill, lemon juice, and olive oil to create a marinade
3. Lay salmon fillets on a baking sheet lined with parchment paper and season lightly with salt and pepper
4. Evenly spoon the marinade over each fillet
5. Bake in the preheated oven for 20 minutes or until salmon is opaque and flakes easily with a fork
6. Remove from oven and allow to cool for a few minutes before serving

Additional Tips:

- Opt for wild-caught salmon for more robust flavors and nutritional benefits compared to farmed
- Dill can be substituted with fresh parsley or cilantro for a different herbal note
- Serve with a side of quinoa and steamed vegetables for a complete meal

Nutritional Values: Calories: 295 kcal, Protein: 23g, Fat: 20g, Saturated Fat: 3g, Carbohydrates: 1g, Sugars: 0g, Fiber: 0g, Sodium: 75mg
SmartPoints Calculation: 7.6

GRILLED CHICKEN BREAST WITH ASPARAGUS

Preparation Time: 10 min
Cooking Time: 15 min
Mode of Cooking: Grilling
Servings: 4
Ingredients:

- 4 skinless chicken breasts (6 oz each)
- 1 lb asparagus, ends trimmed
- 1 Tbsp olive oil
- 2 cloves garlic, minced
- Juice of 1 lemon
- Salt and pepper to taste

Directions:

1. Preheat grill to medium-high heat
2. Lightly coat the chicken breasts and asparagus with olive oil, then season with minced garlic, lemon juice, salt, and pepper
3. Grill chicken breasts for about 6-7 minutes per side or until fully cooked and juices run clear
4. Simultaneously, place asparagus on the grill and cook for about 5-7 minutes, turning occasionally until tender and charred
5. Serve the grilled chicken and asparagus together

Additional Tips:

- Chicken can be marinated in a mixture of yogurt and spices ahead of time for additional moisture and flavor
- Asparagus can be substituted with green beans or zucchini depending on seasonal availability
- Pair this dish with a light kale salad for added fiber and vitamins

Nutritional Values: Calories: 224 kcal, Protein: 29g, Fat: 10g, Saturated Fat: 2g, Carbohydrates: 5g, Sugars: 2g, Fiber: 2g, Sodium: 89mg
SmartPoints Calculation: 4.8

COLORFUL SHRIMP STIR-FRY WITH BROCCOLI AND PEPPERS

Preparation Time: 15 min
Cooking Time: 10 min
Mode of Cooking: Sautéing
Servings: 4
Ingredients:

- 1 lb shrimp, peeled and deveined
- 1 cup broccoli florets
- 1 red bell pepper, sliced
- 1 yellow bell pepper, sliced
- 1 Tbsp olive oil
- 2 Tbsp low sodium soy sauce
- 1 tsp ginger, grated
- 2 cloves garlic, minced
- Salt and pepper to taste

Directions:

1. Heat olive oil in a large skillet over medium-high heat
2. Add garlic and ginger and sauté for 1 min until fragrant
3. Add shrimp and cook for about 2 minutes on each side or until pink and curled
4. Add broccoli and bell peppers to the skillet, stir to combine
5. Pour in soy sauce, season with salt and pepper, and continue to sauté for another 5 minutes until vegetables are tender yet crisp
6. Remove from heat and serve immediately

Additional Tips:

- Try adding a splash of sesame oil for an enhanced flavor profile just before finishing cooking
- Substitute shrimp with tofu for a vegetarian option

- Serve over a bed of brown rice or cauliflower rice to keep it low-carb

Nutritional Values: Calories: 166 kcal, Protein: 24g, Fat: 5g, Saturated Fat: 1g, Carbohydrates: 8g, Sugars: 3g, Fiber: 2g, Sodium: 330mg

SmartPoints Calculation: 3.3

HERBED TURKEY MEATBALLS WITH MARINARA SAUCE

Preparation Time: 20 min
Cooking Time: 30 min
Mode of Cooking: Baking
Servings: 6
Ingredients:
- 1.5 lbs ground turkey
- 1/4 cup breadcrumbs (whole wheat preferred)
- 1/4 cup non-fat Greek yogurt
- 1 egg
- 2 Tbsp fresh parsley, chopped
- 1 tsp dried oregano
- 1/2 cup marinara sauce, low sodium
- Salt and pepper to taste

Directions:
1. Preheat oven to 400°F (200°C)
2. In a large bowl, combine ground turkey, breadcrumbs, Greek yogurt, egg, parsley, oregano, salt, and pepper
3. Mix well and form into 1.5-inch balls
4. Arrange meatballs on a greased baking sheet and bake for 25 minutes
5. In the last 5 minutes of baking, spoon marinara sauce over each meatball
6. Bake until meatballs are cooked through and sauce is bubbly
7. Serve hot

Additional Tips:
- Swap breadcrumbs with rolled oats for an even healthier option
- Add a sprinkle of Parmesan cheese on top of each meatball before serving for those not strictly watching their calorie intake
- Pair with spaghetti squash for a delightful low-carb meal

Nutritional Values: Calories: 180 kcal, Protein: 27g, Fat: 8g, Saturated Fat: 2g, Carbohydrates: 4g, Sugars: 2g, Fiber: 1g, Sodium: 120mg

SmartPoints Calculation: 3.6

ZESTY LIME & HERB TURKEY QUINOA BOWL

Preparation Time: 20 mins
Cooking Time: 25 mins
Mode of Cooking: Sautéing and Boiling
Servings: 4
Ingredients:
- 1 lb ground turkey breast
- 1 cup quinoa
- 2 cups water
- 1 large avocado, diced
- 1 cup cherry tomatoes, halved
- 1/4 cup fresh cilantro, chopped
- 1 Tbsp olive oil
- Zest of 1 lime
- Juice of 2 limes
- 1 tsp ground cumin
- Salt and black pepper to taste

Directions:
1. Rinse the quinoa thoroughly under cold water to remove any bitterness.
2. In a medium saucepan, bring 2 cups of water to a boil, add the quinoa, reduce heat to low, and cook covered for 15 mins until all water is absorbed.
3. While quinoa cooks, heat olive oil in a skillet over medium heat. Add ground turkey and cook until browned. Season with ground cumin, salt, and black pepper.
4. Combine cooked quinoa, cooked turkey, cherry tomatoes, diced avocado, cilantro, lime zest, and lime juice in a large bowl. Mix well to combine flavors.
5. Serve the quinoa bowl immediately, or chill in the refrigerator for a refreshing cold salad.

Additional Tips:
- Swap turkey for chicken for a different protein twist.

- Add a splash of hot sauce or sliced jalapeños for extra heat.
- Double the lime zest for an intensified citrus flavor that pairs wonderfully with the fresh herbs.

Nutritional Values: Calories: 345 kcal, Protein: 27g, Fat: 15g, Saturated Fat: 2g, Carbohydrates: 27g, Sugars: 2g, Fiber: 6g, Sodium: 68mg
SmartPoints Calculation: 8.7

SAVORY SPINACH & MUSHROOM STUFFED BELL PEPPERS

Preparation Time: 15 mins
Cooking Time: 30 mins
Mode of Cooking: Baking
Servings: 4
Ingredients:
- 4 large bell peppers, tops cut, seeds removed
- 1 lb lean ground beef
- 1 cup chopped mushrooms
- 2 cups fresh spinach
- 1 cup cooked brown rice
- 1/4 cup Parmesan cheese, grated
- 1 Tbsp olive oil
- 1 tsp garlic powder
- Salt and black pepper to taste

Directions:
1. Preheat oven to 375°F (190°C).
2. In a skillet, heat olive oil over medium heat. Add ground beef, mushrooms, and garlic powder; cook until beef is thoroughly browned. Stir in spinach until wilted.
3. Mix cooked brown rice and Parmesan cheese into the beef mixture. Season with salt and black pepper.
4. Stuff each bell pepper with the beef and rice mixture, packing it tightly.
5. Place stuffed peppers in a baking dish and cover with foil. Bake in preheated oven for 30 mins.

Additional Tips:
- Use quinoa instead of brown rice for a higher protein option.
- Sprinkle low-fat mozzarella on top during the last 5 mins of baking for a gooey, cheesy finish.
- Serve with a light tomato sauce for added moisture and flavor.

Nutritional Values: Calories: 295 kcal, Protein: 26g, Fat: 13g, Saturated Fat: 4g, Carbohydrates: 20g, Sugars: 5g, Fiber: 4g, Sodium: 180mg
SmartPoints Calculation: 8.1

HERB-INFUSED CHICKEN AND ROOT VEGETABLE ROAST

Preparation Time: 20 mins
Cooking Time: 50 mins
Mode of Cooking: Roasting
Servings: 4
Ingredients:
- 4 skinless chicken breasts
- 1 lb mixed root vegetables (carrots, parsnips, sweet potatoes), cubed
- 3 Tbsp olive oil
- 2 tsp rosemary, chopped
- 2 tsp thyme, chopped
- 4 garlic cloves, minced
- Salt and black pepper to taste

Directions:
1. Preheat oven to 400°F (200°C).
2. Toss the cubed root vegetables with half the olive oil, rosemary, thyme, and garlic in a large roasting pan. Season with salt and pepper.
3. Rub the remaining olive oil and herbs over the chicken breasts and place them on top of the vegetables in the pan.
4. Roast in the preheated oven for 50 mins, or until the chicken is cooked through and the vegetables are tender.

Additional Tips:
- Try different herbs like sage or marjoram to vary the flavor profile.
- For a crispy finish, broil the chicken and vegetables for an additional 2-3 mins at the end of cooking.

- Serve with a side of non-fat Greek yogurt mixed with fresh herbs for a creamy, tangy accompaniment.

Nutritional Values: Calories: 410 kcal, Protein: 35g, Fat: 17g, Saturated Fat: 3g, Carbohydrates: 29g, Sugars: 7g, Fiber: 6g, Sodium: 110mg
SmartPoints Calculation: 10.7

GARLIC LEMON BAKED TILAPIA

Preparation Time: 10 mins
Cooking Time: 15 mins
Mode of Cooking: Baking
Servings: 4
Ingredients:
- 4 tilapia fillets
- 2 Tbsp olive oil
- 4 cloves garlic, minced
- 2 lemons, 1 juiced and 1 sliced
- 2 tsp parsley, chopped
- Salt and black pepper to taste

Directions:
1. Preheat oven to 400°F (200°C).
2. Line a baking sheet with parchment paper and place the tilapia fillets on the sheet.
3. In a small bowl, mix olive oil, lemon juice, minced garlic, and parsley. Season the mixture with salt and black pepper.
4. Pour the garlic lemon mixture over the tilapia and top each fillet with lemon slices.
5. Bake in the preheated oven for 15 mins, or until the fish flakes easily with a fork.

Additional Tips:
- Experiment with other fish like cod or haddock if tilapia is not available.
- Add capers or olives to the baking dish before cooking for a Mediterranean twist.
- Pair with steamed asparagus or green beans for a complete meal.

Nutritional Values: Calories: 195 kcal, Protein: 23g, Fat: 10g, Saturated Fat: 2g, Carbohydrates: 3g
SmartPoints Calculation: 4.2

ZESTY LEMON BASIL TILAPIA

Preparation Time: 10 mins
Cooking Time: 15 mins
Mode of Cooking: Baking
Servings: 4
Ingredients:
- 4 tilapia fillets
- 1 lemon, thinly sliced
- 2 Tbsp fresh basil, chopped
- 2 cloves garlic, minced
- 1 Tbsp olive oil
- Salt and freshly ground black pepper to taste
- 1 tsp dried oregano

Directions:
1. Preheat oven to 375°F (190°C)
2. Line a baking sheet with parchment paper and arrange tilapia fillets in a single layer
3. In a small bowl, combine olive oil, garlic, oregano, salt, and black pepper. Brush this mixture over the tilapia fillets
4. Evenly distribute lemon slices and fresh basil on top of each fillet
5. Bake in the preheated oven until the fish flakes easily with a fork, about 15 mins

Additional Tips:
- For added zest, grate some lemon zest over the fish before baking
- Pair this dish with a side of steamed zero point vegetables like zucchini or spinach for a complete meal
- This recipe can easily be adapted to other firm fish such as cod or haddock

Nutritional Values: Calories: 180 kcal, Protein: 23g, Fat: 5g, Saturated Fat: 1g, Carbohydrates: 3g, Sugars: 0g, Fiber: 1g, Sodium: 120mg
SmartPoints Calculation: 3.5

SPICED CHICKPEA STUFFED BELL PEPPERS

Preparation Time: 20 mins
Cooking Time: 25 mins
Mode of Cooking: Baking
Servings: 4

Ingredients:
- 4 large bell peppers, tops cut, deseeded
- 1 cup chickpeas, drained
- 1 Tbsp olive oil
- 1 small onion, finely diced
- 2 cloves garlic, minced
- 1 tsp cumin
- 1 tsp smoked paprika
- Salt and freshly ground black pepper to taste
- ½ cup chopped fresh parsley
- ¼ cup non-fat Greek yogurt

Directions:
1. Preheat oven to 400°F (204°C)
2. Heat olive oil in a skillet over medium heat. Add onion and garlic and sauté until translucent. Add chickpeas, cumin, smoked paprika, salt, and pepper. Cook for 3-5 mins until flavors meld
3. Stuff each bell pepper with the chickpea mixture. Place in a baking dish and cover with foil
4. Bake for 25 mins. Remove foil, top each pepper with a dollop of Greek yogurt and a sprinkle of fresh parsley before serving

Additional Tips:
- Experiment with different spices such as turmeric or coriander for a new flavor profile
- Serve alongside a quinoa salad for extra protein and fiber
- Yogurt can be flavored with lemon juice or zest for an extra tang

Nutritional Values: Calories: 220 kcal, Protein: 8g, Fat: 5g, Saturated Fat: 1g, Carbohydrates: 34g, Sugars: 8g, Fiber: 9g, Sodium: 150mg

SmartPoints Calculation: 7.2

8.2 VEGETABLE-CENTRIC ENTREES

STUFFED BELL PEPPERS WITH QUINOA AND VEGETABLES

Preparation Time: 20 mins
Cooking Time: 40 mins
Mode of Cooking: Baking
Servings: 4

Ingredients:
- 4 large bell peppers, tops removed and seeds scooped out
- 1 cup quinoa, rinsed
- 2 cups vegetable broth
- 1 medium onion, finely chopped
- 2 cloves garlic, minced
- 1 cup diced zucchini
- 1 cup chopped mushrooms
- 1 cup spinach, chopped
- 2 Tbsp chopped fresh parsley
- 1 tsp dried oregano
- Salt and pepper to taste
- 1 Tbsp olive oil

Directions:
1. Preheat oven to 375°F (190°C).
2. In a saucepan, bring vegetable broth to a boil and add quinoa, simmering until quinoa is tender and broth is absorbed, about 15-20 mins.
3. In a skillet, heat olive oil over medium heat. Add onion and garlic, sauté until translucent. Add zucchini and mushrooms, cooking until vegetables are tender. Stir in spinach, parsley, oregano, salt, and pepper, cooking until spinach is wilted.
4. Combine vegetable mixture with cooked quinoa.
5. Stuff each bell pepper with the quinoa and vegetable mixture. Place stuffed peppers in a baking dish and cover with aluminum foil.
6. Bake in the preheated oven for 30 mins, then remove foil and bake for an additional 10 mins until peppers are tender.

Additional Tips:
- For a cheesy flavor without the cheese, sprinkle nutritional yeast over the stuffed peppers before the final 10 mins of baking.
- Experiment with different vegetables like carrots or celery for varied textures and flavors.

- For added protein, mix in some chopped tofu or shredded, cooked chicken breast to the quinoa mixture.

Nutritional Values: Calories: 220 kcal, Protein: 8g, Fat: 5g, Saturated Fat: 0.7g, Carbohydrates: 37g, Sugars: 6g, Fiber: 7g, Sodium: 300mg

SmartPoints Calculation: 6.8

ROASTED CAULIFLOWER STEAKS WITH CHIMICHURRI SAUCE

Preparation Time: 10 mins
Cooking Time: 25 mins
Mode of Cooking: Baking
Servings: 4
Ingredients:
- 1 large head of cauliflower, sliced into 4 steaks
- 2 Tbsp olive oil
- Salt and pepper to taste
- For the Chimichurri Sauce: 1/2 cup parsley
- 1/4 cup cilantro
- 3 cloves garlic
- 2 Tbsp red wine vinegar
- 1/2 tsp red pepper flakes
- 1/3 cup olive oil
- Salt to taste

Directions:
1. Preheat oven to 425°F (220°C).
2. Brush cauliflower steaks on both sides with olive oil and season with salt and pepper. Place on a baking sheet.
3. Roast in preheated oven until tender and golden, about 25 mins, flipping halfway through.
4. For the Chimichurri Sauce: Blend parsley, cilantro, garlic, red wine vinegar, red pepper flakes, olive oil, and salt in a food processor until smooth.
5. Serve roasted cauliflower steaks drizzled with Chimichurri Sauce.

Additional Tips:
- To ensure even cooking, cut cauliflower steaks from the center of the head to keep them intact.
- Leftover Chimichurri Sauce can be stored in the refrigerator and used as a marinade for meats or a dressing for salads.
- Add a squeeze of lemon for extra zest in the Chimichurri Sauce.

Nutritional Values: Calories: 253 kcal, Protein: 3g, Fat: 21g, Saturated Fat: 3g, Carbohydrates: 14g, Sugars: 4g, Fiber: 5g, Sodium: 200mg

SmartPoints Calculation: 8.7

SPAGHETTI SQUASH WITH TOMATO BASIL SAUCE

Preparation Time: 10 mins
Cooking Time: 45 mins
Mode of Cooking: Baking
Servings: 4
Ingredients:
- 1 large spaghetti squash, halved lengthwise and seeds removed
- 2 cups cherry tomatoes, halved
- 1 onion, finely chopped
- 3 cloves garlic, minced
- 1/4 cup fresh basil, chopped
- 2 Tbsp olive oil
- Salt and pepper to taste
- 1/4 tsp red pepper flakes

Directions:
1. Preheat oven to 400°F (204°C).
2. Place spaghetti squash cut-side down on a baking sheet and bake until tender, about 45 mins.
3. In a skillet, heat 1 Tbsp olive oil over medium heat. Add onion and garlic and sauté until onion is translucent. Add cherry tomatoes and cook until they begin to break down. Stir in basil, salt, pepper, and red pepper flakes.
4. Remove squash from oven, use a fork to scrape out the "spaghetti" strands. Toss spaghetti squash with the tomato basil sauce.

Additional Tips:
- To enhance the flavor, roast a head of garlic alongside the squash, then squeeze the roasted cloves into the tomato sauce.

- For a protein boost, add cooked lentils or chickpeas to the sauce.
- Top with grated Parmesan cheese or nutritional yeast for extra richness.

Nutritional Values: Calories: 162 kcal, Protein: 3g, Fat: 7g, Saturated Fat: 1g, Carbohydrates: 23g, Sugars: 10g, Fiber: 5g, Sodium: 210mg

SmartPoints Calculation: 6.1

GRILLED PORTOBELLO MUSHROOMS WITH BALSAMIC GLAZE

Preparation Time: 10 mins
Cooking Time: 10 mins
Mode of Cooking: Grilling
Servings: 4
Ingredients:
- 4 large Portobello mushrooms, stems removed
- 1/4 cup balsamic vinegar
- 2 Tbsp olive oil
- 1 tsp minced garlic
- Salt and pepper to taste
- 1 Tbsp fresh thyme, chopped

Directions:
1. Preheat grill to medium-high heat.
2. In a bowl, whisk together balsamic vinegar, olive oil, garlic, salt, and pepper. Brush this mixture over both sides of the mushrooms.
3. Grill mushrooms, gill side down, for about 5 mins. Flip, and grill for another 5 mins, or until tender. Sprinkle with fresh thyme to serve.

Additional Tips:
- Use a grill pan if outdoor grilling isn't an option.
- For a savory twist, add a sprinkle of crumbled goat cheese or feta over the mushrooms right before serving.
- To deepen the balsamic flavor, reduce the balsamic vinegar on the stove until thickened into a syrupy consistency before brushing on mushrooms.

Nutritional Values: Calories: 107 kcal, Protein: 2g, Fat: 7g, Saturated Fat: 1g, Carbohydrates: 9g, Sugars: 6g, Fiber: 2g, Sodium: 15mg

SmartPoints Calculation: 4.1

SPICED CAULIFLOWER AND CHICKPEA STEW

Preparation Time: 15 min
Cooking Time: 40 min
Mode of Cooking: Baking
Servings: 6
Ingredients:
- 1 large cauliflower head, cut into florets
- 1 can (15 oz) chickpeas, drained and rinsed
- 1 can (14.5 oz) diced tomatoes
- 1 onion, finely chopped
- 3 cloves garlic, minced
- 1 Tbsp extra virgin olive oil
- 2 tsp ground cumin
- 1 tsp turmeric powder
- 1 tsp smoked paprika
- 1 qt vegetable broth
- Salt and pepper to taste
- Fresh cilantro for garnish

Directions:
1. Preheat oven to 400°F (200°C)
2. Toss cauliflower florets, chickpeas, onion, and garlic with olive oil, cumin, turmeric, and paprika in a large baking dish
3. Bake in preheated oven for 30 min, stirring halfway through
4. Remove from oven and stir in diced tomatoes and vegetable broth
5. Return to oven and bake for an additional 10 min
6. Season with salt and pepper
7. Garnish with fresh cilantro before serving.

Additional Tips:
- Use low-sodium vegetable broth to control the salt content, making it heart-healthier
- Chickpeas can be substituted with lentils or beans for variety
- Add a squeeze of lemon juice before serving to enhance flavors
- Serve with a side of whole-grain flatbread for a hearty meal

Nutritional Values: Calories: 180 kcal, Protein: 8g, Fat: 5g, Saturated Fat: 1g, Carbohydrates: 28g, Sugars: 7g, Fiber: 9g, Sodium: 800mg

SmartPoints Calculation: 5.8

SESAME GINGER TOFU STIR-FRY

Preparation Time: 10 min
Cooking Time: 20 min
Mode of Cooking: Sautéing
Servings: 4
Ingredients:
- 14 oz firm tofu, pressed and cubed
- 1 bell pepper, thinly sliced
- 1 cup snap peas
- 2 carrots, julienned
- 1 Tbsp sesame oil
- 2 Tbsp soy sauce, low sodium
- 1 Tbsp fresh ginger, grated
- 2 garlic cloves, minced
- 1 Tbsp sesame seeds
- 2 green onions, sliced

Directions:
1. Heat sesame oil in a large skillet over medium-high heat
2. Add tofu cubes and sauté until golden brown, about 10 min
3. Remove tofu and set aside
4. In the same skillet, add bell pepper, snap peas, and carrots, sauté for about 5 min
5. Return tofu to the skillet
6. Stir in soy sauce, ginger, and garlic, cook for another 5 min
7. Remove from heat, sprinkle with sesame seeds and green onions.

Additional Tips:
- Opt for firm tofu for better texture and easier handling
- Julienne the carrots for quicker, even cooking
- Garnish with additional sesame seeds for a nuttier flavor and appealing presentation
- To enhance flavor, marinate tofu in soy sauce and ginger mixture for at least 30 min before cooking

Nutritional Values: Calories: 150 kcal, Protein: 10g, Fat: 8g, Saturated Fat: 1g, Carbohydrates: 10g, Sugars: 4g, Fiber: 3g, Sodium: 300mg

SmartPoints Calculation: 4.4

BAKED SPINACH AND ARTICHOKE HEARTS

Preparation Time: 10 min
Cooking Time: 22 min
Mode of Cooking: Baking
Servings: 5
Ingredients:
- 2 cups fresh spinach, chopped
- 1 can (14 oz) artichoke hearts, drained and chopped
- 1 cup non-fat Greek yogurt
- 2 cloves garlic, minced
- 1/2 cup Parmesan cheese, grated
- Salt and pepper to taste
- 1 tsp olive oil for greasing

Directions:
1. Preheat oven to 375°F (190°C)
2. Mix spinach, artichoke hearts, Greek yogurt, garlic, and half of the Parmesan cheese in a bowl
3. Season with salt and pepper
4. Grease a baking dish with olive oil
5. Transfer the mixture to the greased dish
6. Sprinkle remaining Parmesan on top
7. Bake in preheated oven for about 22 min or until top is golden and bubbly.

Additional Tips:
- Substitute Greek yogurt with low-fat sour cream for a different flavor profile
- Add a pinch of nutmeg or cayenne pepper for an extra kick
- This dish can also be served as a dip with whole-wheat pita chips or fresh vegetables
- Ensure to drain artichokes well to avoid a watery dish

Nutritional Values: Calories: 120 kcal, Protein: 8g, Fat: 4g, Saturated Fat: 2g, Carbohydrates: 12g, Sugars: 3g, Fiber: 4g, Sodium: 320mg
SmartPoints Calculation: 3.8

ROASTED EGGPLANT WITH TOMATO RELISH

Preparation Time: 15 min
Cooking Time: 25 min

Mode of Cooking: Roasting
Servings: 4
Ingredients:
- 2 medium eggplants, sliced into 1/2-inch thick rounds
- 2 large tomatoes, finely chopped
- 1 onion, finely diced
- 3 Tbsp chopped fresh basil
- 1 Tbsp balsamic vinegar
- 2 Tbsp olive oil
- Salt and pepper to taste
- Fresh parsley for garnish

Directions:
1. Preheat oven to 425°F (220°C)
2. Arrange eggplant rounds on a baking sheet
3. Brush each round with olive oil and season with salt and pepper
4. Roast in the oven for 25 min
5. While eggplants are roasting, combine tomatoes, onion, basil, and balsamic vinegar in a bowl
6. Once eggplants are done, top with tomato relish
7. Garnish with fresh parsley.

Additional Tips:
- Use different types of tomatoes for a more vibrant and flavorful relish
- Eggplant rounds can be sprinkled with a bit of Parmesan before roasting for a cheesy flavor
- For a smoky taste, grill the eggplant instead of roasting
- This dish pairs well with grilled chicken or fish for a complete meal

Nutritional Values: Calories: 140 kcal, Protein: 2g, Fat: 7g, Saturated Fat: 1g, Carbohydrates: 19g, Sugars: 9g, Fiber: 6g, Sodium: 10mg
SmartPoints Calculation: 5.4

SAVORY SPINACH AND ARTICHOKE GALETTES

Preparation Time: 15 min
Cooking Time: 25 min
Mode of Cooking: Baking
Servings: 6
Ingredients:
- 1 1/2 cups whole wheat pastry flour
- 1/2 tsp salt
- 1/2 cup nonfat Greek yogurt
- 1/4 cup ice water
- 2 Tbsp olive oil
- 1 medium onion, thinly sliced
- 2 garlic cloves, minced
- 4 cups fresh spinach
- 1 cup canned artichoke hearts, drained and chopped
- 1/2 cup grated Parmesan cheese
- Fresh lemon zest from 1 lemon
- Salt and pepper to taste

Directions:
1. Combine Flour and Seasonings: In a large bowl, mix the whole wheat pastry flour and salt.
2. Make the Dough: Stir in the nonfat Greek yogurt and ice water to form a smooth dough. Divide into 6 balls and chill for 10 min.
3. Sauté Vegetables: In a skillet, heat olive oil over medium heat, add onion and garlic, cook until translucent. Add spinach and cook until wilted.
4. Prepare Filling: Combine sautéed veggies, chopped artichokes, Parmesan cheese, lemon zest, salt, and pepper in a bowl.
5. Assemble Galettes: On a floured surface, roll each ball into a 7-inch circle. Spoon the vegetable mix onto each, leaving a 1-inch border. Fold edges over the filling, pleating to hold it in.
6. Bake: Preheat oven to 400°F (204°C). Bake galettes on a lined baking sheet for 25 min until golden.

Additional Tips:
- Use Gluten-Free Flour for allergies.
- Create a Vegan Version: Substitute nonfat Greek yogurt with a non-dairy yogurt and Parmesan cheese with nutritional yeast.

- Add a Protein Boost: Include chickpeas or shredded skinless chicken breast to the filling for an extra protein hit.
- Lemon Zest Tip: Use a fine grater for the zest to avoid bitter white pith.

Nutritional Values: Calories: 194 kcal, Protein: 9g, Fat: 6g, Saturated Fat: 2g, Carbohydrates: 28g, Sugars: 2g, Fiber: 5g, Sodium: 370mg
SmartPoints Calculation: 5.8

CURRIED CAULIFLOWER WITH LENTILS

Preparation Time: 10 min
Cooking Time: 20 min
Mode of Cooking: Sautéing
Servings: 4
Ingredients:
- 1 Tbsp olive oil
- 1 large onion, chopped
- 2 cloves garlic, minced
- 1 Tbsp grated ginger
- 2 Tbsp curry powder
- 1 head cauliflower, cut into florets
- 1 cup red lentils
- 4 cups vegetable broth
- 1 cup chopped tomatoes
- Fresh cilantro for garnish
- Salt to taste

Directions:
1. Prepare Ingredients: Heat olive oil in a large pan over medium heat, then add onion, garlic, and ginger and fry until onion is soft.
2. Add Spices: Stir in curry powder, cooking for 1 min until fragrant.
3. Add Main Ingredients: Incorporate cauliflower, lentils, and vegetable broth, bringing to a boil.
4. Simmer: Reduce heat and simmer for 20 min, until lentils are tender. Stir in chopped tomatoes and cook for another 2 min.
5. Finish & Serve: Season with salt, garnish with fresh cilantro, and serve warm.

Additional Tips:
- Quick-Prep Tip: Use pre-chopped cauliflower to save prep time.
- For a Creamier Texture: Stir in a spoonful of non-fat Greek yogurt before serving.
- Additional Spice: Add a pinch of chili flakes for extra heat if desired.
- Leftover Makeover: Use any leftovers as a savory filling for wraps or pita bread.

Nutritional Values: Calories: 235 kcal, Protein: 14g, Fat: 4g, Saturated Fat: 0.5g, Carbohydrates: 36g, Sugars: 6g, Fiber: 15g, Sodium: 300mg
SmartPoints Calculation: 6.7

8.3 ONE-POT AND SHEET PAN DINNERS

ONE-POT CHICKEN AND QUINOA WITH SPINACH

Preparation Time: 15 mins
Cooking Time: 30 mins
Mode of Cooking: Sautéing and Simmering
Servings: 4
Ingredients:
- 1 lb boneless skinless chicken breasts, cut into bite-sized pieces
- 1 cup uncooked quinoa
- 2 cups low-sodium chicken broth
- 1 onion, diced
- 1 garlic clove, minced
- 3 cups baby spinach
- 1 tsp olive oil
- 1 tsp paprika
- Salt and pepper to taste

Directions:
1. Instructions: Heat olive oil in a deep pot over medium heat.
2. Add diced onion and minced garlic, sauté until onion is translucent.
3. Add chicken pieces, sprinkle with paprika, salt, and pepper, and cook until chicken is lightly browned on all sides.
4. Pour in quinoa and chicken broth, stir to combine.

5. Bring the mixture to a boil, then reduce heat to low and cover the pot. Simmer for 20 mins or until quinoa is cooked and liquid is absorbed.
6. Stir in baby spinach and cover the pot. Let it sit for 5 mins or until spinach is wilted.
7. Serve hot, garnished with a lemon wedge if desired.

Additional Tips:
- Additional To make this dish vegetarian, substitute the chicken with tofu or chickpeas.
- Intensify flavors with a dash of crushed red pepper flakes.
- For a refreshing twist, add a sprinkle of lemon zest before serving.
- This recipe is even better the next day, making great leftovers for lunch.

Nutritional Values: Calories: 295 kcal, Protein: 28g, Fat: 8g, Saturated Fat: 1.5g, Carbohydrates: 27g, Sugars: 2g, Fiber: 4g, Sodium: 150mg
SmartPoints Calculation: 6.9

SHEET PAN BAKED COD WITH VEGETABLES

Preparation Time: 10 mins
Cooking Time: 20 mins
Mode of Cooking: Baking
Servings: 4
Ingredients:
- 4 cod fillets, about 6 oz each
- 2 bell peppers, sliced
- 1 zucchini, sliced
- 1/2 red onion, sliced
- 12 cherry tomatoes
- 2 Tbsp olive oil
- 1 lemon, sliced
- 1 tsp dried thyme
- Salt and pepper to taste

Directions:
1. Instructions: Preheat the oven to 400°F (200°C).
2. On a large baking sheet, place cod fillets in the center, surrounded by sliced bell peppers, zucchini, red onion, and cherry tomatoes.
3. Drizzle olive oil over the fish and vegetables, and then sprinkle with dried thyme, salt, and pepper.
4. Top each fillet with a slice of lemon.
5. Bake in the oven for 20 mins or until the vegetables are tender and the cod is flaky.
6. Serve immediately, garnished with fresh parsley if desired.

Additional Tips:
- Additional For a spicy kick, sprinkle some chili flakes over the vegetables before baking.
- Baking paper can be used for easier cleanup.
- Experiment with different herbs like basil or oregano for variation in flavor.
- Serve with a side of quinoa or a fresh green salad for a complete meal.

Nutritional Values: Calories: 230 kcal, Protein: 23g, Fat: 10g, Saturated Fat: 1.5g, Carbohydrates: 12g, Sugars: 6g, Fiber: 3g, Sodium: 90mg
SmartPoints Calculation: 5.9

ONE-POT TURKEY CHILI WITH BEANS

Preparation Time: 20 mins
Cooking Time: 45 mins
Mode of Cooking: Simmering
Servings: 6
Ingredients:
- 1 lb ground turkey
- 1 can (15 oz) black beans, drained and rinsed
- 1 can (15 oz) diced tomatoes
- 1 onion, diced
- 2 garlic cloves, minced
- 2 cups low-sodium vegetable broth
- 1 bell pepper, chopped
- 1 Tbsp chili powder
- 1 tsp cumin
- 1 tsp olive oil
- Salt and pepper to taste

Directions:
1. Instructions: Heat olive oil in a large pot over medium heat.
2. Add diced onion and minced garlic, sauté until the onion is translucent.

3. Add ground turkey, cook until browned and no longer pink.
4. Stir in chili powder and cumin, mix well.
5. Add black beans, diced tomatoes, chopped bell pepper, and vegetable broth.
6. Bring to a boil, then reduce heat and simmer for 45 mins, stirring occasionally.
7. Season with salt and pepper to taste.
8. Serve hot, garnished with chopped cilantro and a dollop of non-fat Greek yogurt if desired.

Additional Tips:
- Additional Use lean ground turkey to reduce fat content.
- Add corn or other vegetables for additional nutrition and flavor.
- For a thicker chili, mash some of the beans before adding them to the pot.

Nutritional Values: Calories: 295 kcal, Protein: 22g, Fat: 8g, Saturated Fat: 2g, Carbohydrates: 32g, Sugars: 5g, Fiber: 8g, Sodium: 480mg
SmartPoints Calculation: 8

Roasted Salmon and Fennel with Citrus Herb Sauce

Preparation Time: 15 min
Cooking Time: 25 min
Mode of Cooking: Baking
Servings: 4
Ingredients:
- 4 salmon fillets, about 6 oz each
- 2 medium fennel bulbs, thinly sliced
- 1 large orange, zested and juiced
- 2 Tbsp extra virgin olive oil
- 1 Tbsp chopped fresh dill
- 1 Tbsp chopped fresh parsley
- 1 tsp Dijon mustard
- Salt and freshly ground black pepper to taste

Directions:
1. Preheat oven to 400°F (200°C)
2. Place salmon and fennel in a single layer on a baking sheet lined with parchment paper
3. Drizzle with 1 Tbsp olive oil and season with salt and pepper
4. Bake for 20-25 min, or until salmon is cooked through and fennel is tender and golden
5. In a small bowl, whisk together orange juice, zest, remaining olive oil, dill, parsley, and mustard to create the citrus herb sauce
6. Once salmon and fennel are done, spoon citrus herb sauce over the top before serving

Additional Tips:
- Prepare sauce while salmon cooks to save time
- Fennel can be replaced by thinly sliced bell peppers or carrots for a different flavor profile
- Increase citrus intensity by adding lemon zest to the sauce

Nutritional Values: Calories: 355 kcal, Protein: 23g, Fat: 12g, Saturated Fat: 1.8g, Carbohydrates: 10g, Sugars: 8g, Fiber: 3g, Sodium: 95mg
SmartPoints Calculation: 10

Spicy Paprika and Garlic Shrimp

Preparation Time: 10 min
Cooking Time: 6 min
Mode of Cooking: Baking
Servings: 4
Ingredients:
- 1 lb large shrimp, peeled and deveined
- 3 cloves garlic, minced
- 1 Tbsp smoked paprika
- 2 tsp olive oil
- 1 tsp chili flakes
- Salt and black pepper to taste

Directions:
1. Preheat oven to 450°F (230°C)
2. In a medium bowl, toss the shrimp with garlic, smoked paprika, chili flakes, olive oil, salt, and black pepper
3. Spread shrimp in a single layer on a lined baking sheet
4. Bake for 5-6 min, or just until shrimp are pink and cooked through

Additional Tips:
- Use parchment paper for easy cleanup

- For less heat, reduce the chili flakes by half
- Serve over a bed of zero point spinach leaves tossed with lemon juice for a complete meal

Nutritional Values: Calories: 120 kcal, Protein: 23g, Fat: 3g, Saturated Fat: 0.5g, Carbohydrates: 2g, Sugars: 0g, Fiber: 1g, Sodium: 117mg

SmartPoints Calculation: 1.5

LEMON THYME CHICKEN

Preparation Time: 20 min
Cooking Time: 50 min
Mode of Cooking: Baking
Servings: 4
Ingredients:

- 4 skinless bone-in chicken thighs
- 4 cloves garlic, minced
- 1 lemon, zested and juiced
- 2 Tbsp olive oil
- 2 Tbsp fresh thyme leaves
- Salt and black pepper to taste
- ½ cup low-sodium chicken broth

Directions:

1. Preheat oven to 375°F (190°C)
2. In a large bowl, combine garlic, lemon zest, lemon juice, olive oil, thyme, salt, and black pepper
3. Toss chicken thighs in the mixture until evenly coated
4. Arrange chicken in a baking dish and pour over any remaining herb mixture along with chicken broth
5. Bake for 45-50 min, or until chicken reaches an internal temperature of 165°F (74°C)

Additional Tips:

- Rub the herb mixture under the skin for deeper flavor penetration
- Use fresh rosemary instead of thyme for a different herbal note
- Pair with steamed green beans for a complete zero point meal

Nutritional Values: Calories: 290 kcal, Protein: 33g, Fat: 16g, Saturated Fat: 3g, Carbohydrates: 4g, Sugars: 1g, Fiber: 1g, Sodium: 95mg

SmartPoints Calculation: 6.6

MEDITERRANEAN VEGETABLE AND CHICKPEA STEW

Preparation Time: 20 min
Cooking Time: 40 min
Mode of Cooking: Baking
Servings: 4
Ingredients:

- 1 medium onion, chopped
- 2 carrots, peeled and sliced
- 2 stalks celery, sliced
- 3 cloves garlic, minced
- 1 red bell pepper, chopped
- 1 zucchini, chopped
- 15 oz can chickpeas, drained and rinsed
- 14 oz can diced tomatoes
- 1 tsp dried oregano
- 2 Tbsp olive oil
- Salt and black pepper to taste
- Fresh parsley for garnish

Directions:

1. Preheat oven to 375°F (190°C)
2. In a large oven-proof pot, sauté onion, carrots, celery, and garlic in olive oil until slightly softened
3. Add bell pepper, zucchini, chickpeas, diced tomatoes, oregano, salt, and black pepper, stirring to combine
4. Cover and bake in the oven for 35-40 min, or until vegetables are tender
5. Garnish with fresh parsley before serving

Additional Tips:

- Experiment with different vegetables like eggplant or squash
- Add a pinch of chili flakes for a spicy kick
- Serve with a side of whole wheat pita bread for extra heartiness

Nutritional Values: Calories: 265 kcal, Protein: 9g, Fat: 10g, Saturated Fat: 1.4g, Carbohydrates: 35g, Sugars: 11g, Fiber: 9g, Sodium: 300mg

SmartPoints Calculation: 8.9

LEMONGRASS INFUSED TILAPIA BAKE

Preparation Time: 15 min
Cooking Time: 25 min
Mode of Cooking: Baking
Servings: 4
Ingredients:
- 4 tilapia fillets
- 2 lemongrass stalks (minced)
- 1 inch of ginger (grated)
- 1 garlic clove (minced)
- 1 red bell pepper (sliced thinly)
- 1 small red onion (sliced)
- 1 lemon (juiced and zested)
- 1 Tbsp olive oil
- Salt and pepper to taste

Directions:
1. Instructions: Preheat your oven to 375°F (190°C)
2. In a bowl, mix olive oil, lemongrass, ginger, garlic, lemon juice, and zest for a marinade
3. Arrange the tilapia in a baking dish and scatter the onions and bell peppers around the fish
4. Pour the marinade evenly over the fish ensuring all pieces are well coated
5. Bake in the oven for 25 minutes or until the fish flakes easily with a fork

Additional Tips:
- Additional Marinate the fish for up to an hour before baking for more robust flavors
- Use parchment paper in the baking dish for easier cleanup
- Serve with a side of steamed quinoa or brown rice for a complete meal

Nutritional Values: Calories: 172 kcal, Protein: 23g, Fat: 6g, Saturated Fat: 1g, Carbohydrates: 5g, Sugars: 2g, Fiber: 1g, Sodium: 67mg
SmartPoints Calculation: 3.5

SMOKY PAPRIKA CHICKEN SKILLET

Preparation Time: 20 min
Cooking Time: 30 min
Mode of Cooking: Sautéing
Servings: 4
Ingredients:
- 4 skinless chicken breasts
- 1 Tbsp smoked paprika
- 2 Tbsp light olive oil
- 1 large onion (diced)
- 2 cloves garlic (minced)
- 1 cup cherry tomatoes
- 1 cup zucchini (sliced)
- 1/2 cup red wine (optional)
- Salt and black pepper to taste

Directions:
1. Instructions: Heat olive oil over medium heat in a large skillet
2. Sauté the onion and garlic until translucent
3. Season the chicken with salt, pepper, and smoked paprika, add to the skillet, and cook until browned on both sides
4. Add cherry tomatoes, zucchini, and red wine (if using), covering the skillet and letting it simmer for about 20 minutes or until the chicken is cooked through and vegetables are tender

Additional Tips:
- Additional Substitute red wine with chicken broth if preferred
- Sprinkle with fresh herbs like parsley or cilantro before serving for added color and flavor
- Pair with a simple leafy green salad

Nutritional Values: Calories: 265 kcal, Protein: 28g, Fat: 10g, Saturated Fat: 2g, Carbohydrates: 9g, Sugars: 5g, Fiber: 2g, Sodium: 200mg
SmartPoints Calculation: 6.5

HERBED LEMON SHRIMP AND ASPARAGUS

Preparation Time: 10 min
Cooking Time: 12 min
Mode of Cooking: Grilling
Servings: 4
Ingredients:
- 1 lb shrimp (peeled and deveined)
- 1 bunch of asparagus (trimmed)
- 2 lemons (one sliced, one juiced)

- 2 Tbsp parsley (chopped)
- 1 Tbsp olive oil
- Salt and black pepper to taste

Directions:

1. Instructions: Preheat the grill to medium-high heat
2. Toss the shrimp and asparagus in olive oil, lemon juice, salt, and black pepper
3. Lay lemon slices across the grill and place shrimp and asparagus on top
4. Grill for about 6 minutes per side or until the shrimp are opaque and the asparagus is tender-crisp
5. Remove from grill and sprinkle with chopped parsley

Additional Tips:

- Additional For a zestier flavor, add lemon zest to the marinade
- Grill with sprigs of fresh rosemary for a smokey herbaceous note
- Serve over a bed of light couscous or mixed greens

Nutritional Values: Calories: 197 kcal, Protein: 24g, Fat: 8g, Saturated Fat: 1g, Carbohydrates: 7g, Sugars: 3g, Fiber: 3g, Sodium: 117mg

SmartPoints Calculation: 4.3

CHAPTER 9: GUILT-FREE ZERO POINT SNACKS AND DESSERTS

Who says you can't indulge in scrumptious snacks and desserts while on a journey to weight loss? If you've ever felt pangs of guilt reaching for that second cookie or doubted your choice of an evening snack, this chapter is here to revolutionize your outlook. Welcome to the delicious world of guilt-free, zero point snacks and desserts—an oasis where flavor meets health without compromise.

Imagine returning home after a long day, your energy spent and your stomach grumbling. The usual suspects might tempt you—perhaps a bag of chips or a sugary treat—but what if you could satisfy your cravings without derailing your wellness goals? That's not only possible; it's enjoyable with the recipes you'll discover here. From creamy avocado chocolate pudding to crispy kale chips seasoned with your favorite spices, each recipe encapsulates pleasure without the guilt.

During my years as a wellness coach, I've witnessed the transformation in my clients when they discover they can enjoy their favorite flavors in a healthier format. Take Sarah, for instance, a busy mother of two. Her evenings were battles against unhealthy snack cravings until she experimented with zero point recipes. She shared with delight how her family now rushes to the kitchen, not for store-bought cookies, but for her freshly baked oatmeal banana cookies which are both nutritious and simply delectable.

We all know that sticking to a diet can be tough when the recommended foods are bland or uninspiring. My aim with these snacks and desserts is to break this stereotype by infusing zest, sweetness, and spice back into dishes that boost your energy without the calorie burden. Every recipe here is crafted to ensure that you never have to question whether you're treating yourself too much or stepping outside your dietary boundaries.

Incorporating these dishes into your routine is about celebrating food's natural richness and your dedication to a healthier lifestyle harmoniously. It's time to set aside your reservations and embrace the joy of snacking with excitement and zero guilt. Let's dive into flavors that excite the palate and nourish the body, proving once and for all that healthy eating doesn't need to be flavorless or restrictive!

9.1 SAVORY SNACKS TO CURB CRAVINGS

SPICED TURMERIC ROASTED CHICKPEAS

Preparation Time: 10 min
Cooking Time: 25 min
Mode of Cooking: Baking
Servings: 4

Ingredients:
- 15 oz can of chickpeas
- 1 Tbsp olive oil
- 1 tsp turmeric powder
- 1 tsp smoked paprika
- 1/2 tsp garlic powder
- 1/4 tsp cayenne pepper
- Salt to taste

Directions:

1. Rinse and drain the chickpeas before patting them thoroughly dry to remove excess moisture.
2. Preheat oven to 400°F (200°C).
3. In a bowl, combine olive oil, turmeric, smoked paprika, garlic powder, cayenne pepper, and salt. Add chickpeas and toss until evenly coated.

4. Spread the chickpeas on a baking sheet in a single layer.
5. Bake in the preheated oven for about 25 min until crispy and golden, stirring halfway through to ensure even roasting.

Additional Tips:

• Experiment with Different Spices: Feel free to adjust the spice blend to suit your taste preferences or try other spices like cumin or chili powder.

• Storage Tip: Store the roasted chickpeas in an airtight container to maintain their crunch for a few days.

• Serving Suggestion: Serve these as a snack or toss them into a salad for added texture and flavor.

Nutritional Values: Calories: 130 kcal, Protein: 5g, Fat: 5g, Saturated Fat: 0.5g, Carbohydrates: 17g, Sugars: 0g, Fiber: 5g, Sodium: 200mg

SmartPoints Calculation: 3.6

COOL CUCUMBER YOGURT BITES

Preparation Time: 15 min
Cooking Time: none
Mode of Cooking: No Cooking
Servings: 4
Ingredients:
- 1 large cucumber
- 1 cup non-fat Greek yogurt
- 2 Tbsp fresh dill, finely chopped
- Lemon zest from 1 lemon
- 1 clove garlic, minced
- Salt and pepper to taste

Directions:

1. Slice cucumber into 1/2-inch thick rounds.
2. In a mixing bowl, combine Greek yogurt, chopped dill, lemon zest, minced garlic, salt, and pepper. Mix until well blended.
3. Dollop a spoonful of the yogurt mixture onto each cucumber slice and spread lightly.

Additional Tips:

• Use Different Herbs: Substitute dill with mint or basil for a different flavor profile.

• Make It Zesty: Add a splash of lemon juice to the yogurt mixture for extra tang.

• Advance Preparation: Prepare the yogurt mixture in advance and store in the refrigerator; assemble bites just before serving to ensure the cucumbers remain crisp.

Nutritional Values: Calories: 40 kcal, Protein: 6g, Fat: 0g, Saturated Fat: 0g, Carbohydrates: 4g, Sugars: 2g, Fiber: 0g, Sodium: 50mg

SmartPoints Calculation: 0.9

SAVORY EGG & SEA SALT SNACKERS

Preparation Time: 10 min
Cooking Time: 10 min
Mode of Cooking: Boiling
Servings: 6
Ingredients:
- 6 large eggs
- Sea salt to taste
- Freshly cracked black pepper to taste
- Paprika for garnish

Directions:

1. Place eggs in a saucepan and cover with water. Bring to a boil and then simmer for 10 min. Remove from heat and cool in an ice bath.
2. Once cooled, peel the eggs and cut them in half.
3. Sprinkle with sea salt, cracked black pepper, and a light dusting of paprika before serving.

Additional Tips:

• Boiling Tip: Add a pinch of baking soda to the water to make the eggs easier to peel.

• Creative Serving: Use a small cookie cutter to shape egg slices for a fun presentation.

• Add-Ons: For added flavor, sprinkle some chopped chives or a dash of hot sauce on top of the eggs.

Nutritional Values: Calories: 70 kcal, Protein: 6g, Fat: 5g, Saturated Fat: 1.5g, Carbohydrates: 1g, Sugars: 0g, Fiber: 0g, Sodium: 62mg

SmartPoints Calculation: 2

PARMESAN ZUCCHINI CHIPS

Preparation Time: 10 min
Cooking Time: 20 min
Mode of Cooking: Baking
Servings: 4
Ingredients:
- 2 large zucchini
- 1/4 cup grated Parmesan cheese
- 1 Tbsp olive oil
- 1/4 tsp garlic powder
- Salt and pepper to taste

Directions:
1. Preheat oven to 450°F (230°C).
2. Slice zucchini into 1/4-inch thick rounds.
3. In a bowl, toss zucchini slices with olive oil, garlic powder, salt, and pepper.
4. Arrange slices in a single layer on a baking sheet and sprinkle with grated Parmesan.
5. Bake for about 20 min until crispy and golden brown.

Additional Tips:
- Slice Uniformity: Ensure all zucchini slices are the same thickness for even baking.
- Parmesan Swap: Try using other hard cheeses like Asiago or Pecorino Romano for different flavors.
- Crispness Tip: For extra crispy chips, let them cool on the baking sheet before serving.

Nutritional Values: Calories: 90 kcal, Protein: 4g, Fat: 7g, Saturated Fat: 2g, Carbohydrates: 3g, Sugars: 2g, Fiber: 1g, Sodium: 115mg
SmartPoints Calculation: 3.1

ZESTY LIME SHRIMP CEVICHE

Preparation Time: 20 mins
Cooking Time: No Cooking
Mode of Cooking: Grilling (optional for shrimp)
Servings: 4
Ingredients:
- 1 lb. raw shrimp, peeled and deveined
- 1 cup fresh lime juice
- 1/2 cup diced red onion
- 1/2 cup chopped fresh cilantro
- 1 cup diced tomatoes
- 1 diced avocado
- 1 minced jalapeño (seeded for less heat)
- Salt to taste

Directions:
1. Prepare the Ingredients: Dice shrimp into half-inch pieces. Mix in a bowl with lime juice ensuring shrimp are completely submerged. Let marinate in refrigerator for 12-15 mins until they appear opaque and cooked.
2. Combine Other Ingredients: In another bowl, combine red onion, cilantro, tomatoes, avocado, and jalapeño.
3. Mix and Season: Once shrimp are marinated, combine them with the vegetable mix. Add salt to taste.
4. Serve Chilled: Serve ceviche cold, garnished with extra cilantro or lime wedges.

Additional Tips:
- Grill Option for Shrimp: For added flavor, quickly grill shrimp before dicing and marinating.
- Adjust Heat: Use more or less jalapeño according to heat preference. Removing seeds reduces spiciness.
- Lime Juice Tip: Use enough lime juice to cover shrimp for even 'cooking' in the acid.

Nutritional Values: Calories: 180 kcal, Protein: 24g, Fat: 8g, Saturated Fat: 1.5g, Carbohydrates: 9g, Sugars: 3g, Fiber: 3g, Sodium: 300mg
SmartPoints Calculation: 3.9

SMOKED SALMON AND CUCUMBER ROLLS

Preparation Time: 15 mins
Cooking Time: No Cooking
Mode of Cooking: No Cooking
Servings: 6
Ingredients:
- 12 oz. smoked salmon
- 2 English cucumbers
- 1/2 cup non-fat Greek yogurt
- 1 Tbsp fresh dill, chopped
- 1 Tbsp lemon juice
- Black pepper to taste

Directions:
1. Prepare the Ingredients: Slice cucumbers lengthwise using a mandoline for even thin slices.
2. Mix Filling: Combine Greek yogurt, dill, and lemon juice in a bowl. Season with black pepper.
3. Assemble Rolls: Spread a thin layer of yogurt mixture over each cucumber slice, then top with a slice of smoked salmon. Roll tightly.
4. Chill and Serve: Refrigerate rolls for about 10 mins before serving to firm up.

Additional Tips:
- Upright Presentation: Serve rolls standing upright on a platter, secured with a toothpick.
- Dill Substitute: If fresh dill is unavailable, use dried dill but reduce the amount by half.
- Squeeze of Elegance: Enhance flavor by adding a small squeeze of fresh lemon juice over each roll before serving.

Nutritional Values: Calories: 100 kcal, Protein: 15g, Fat: 4g, Saturated Fat: 1g, Carbohydrates: 3g, Sugars: 2g, Fiber: 1g, Sodium: 670mg
SmartPoints Calculation: 2.1

HERBED TOFU AND VEGGIE SKEWERS

Preparation Time: 25 mins
Cooking Time: 10 mins
Mode of Cooking: Grilling
Servings: 4
Ingredients:
- 1 lb. firm tofu, cubed
- 1 zucchini, cut into rounds
- 1 bell pepper, cut into pieces
- 1 red onion, cut into wedges
- 1 Tbsp olive oil
- 2 Tbsp mixed herbs (thyme, oregano, basil)
- Salt and pepper to taste

Directions:
1. Prepare Ingredients: Press tofu between paper towels to remove excess moisture. Cut vegetables into uniform pieces to ensure even cooking.
2. Marinate: Toss tofu and vegetables with olive oil, mixed herbs, and seasoning. Let sit for 15 mins.
3. Skewer and Grill: Thread tofu and vegetables alternately on skewers. Grill over medium heat for 10 mins, turning occasionally.
4. Serve Hot: Serve skewers hot, optionally drizzled with a squeeze of fresh lemon or balsamic glaze.

Additional Tips:
- Tofu Pressing Tip: For firmer tofu, press under a weight for at least 30 mins before marinating.
- Herb Variations: Experiment with different herbs like rosemary or cilantro for varied flavors.
- Serving Suggestion: Serve over a bed of quinoa for a complete meal.

Nutritional Values: Calories: 150 kcal, Protein: 10g, Fat: 9g, Saturated Fat: 1.5g, Carbohydrates: 8g, Sugars: 4g, Fiber: 2g, Sodium: 30mg
SmartPoints Calculation: 4.5

BEETROOT AND FETA CHEESE DIP

Preparation Time: 15 mins
Cooking Time: none
Mode of Cooking: No Cooking
Servings: 8
Ingredients:
- 3 medium beetroots, roasted and peeled
- 1 cup non-fat Greek yogurt
- 1/2 cup crumbled feta cheese
- 2 cloves garlic, minced
- 1 Tbsp lemon juice
- Salt and pepper to taste
- Extra virgin olive oil for drizzling

Directions:
1. Prepare the Ingredients: Puree roasted beetroots in a food processor until smooth.
2. Combine with Other Ingredients: Add Greek yogurt, feta cheese, minced garlic, and lemon juice to beetroot puree and blend until well combined. Season with salt and pepper.
3. Chill: Refrigerate dip for at least 1 hr before serving to enhance flavors.

4. Serve: Serve chilled with a drizzle of olive oil over the top.

Additional Tips:
- Color Pop: Garnish with chopped herbs like parsley or chives to add a splash of color.
- Garlic Adjustment: Use roasted garlic instead of raw for a milder, sweeter flavor.
- Olive Oil Finish: Top with a high-quality olive oil for a rich, luxurious finish to the dish.

Nutritional Values: Calories: 90 kcal, Protein: 5g, Fat: 4g, Saturated Fat: 2g, Carbohydrates: 9g, Sugars: 7g, Fiber: 2g, Sodium: 200mg

SmartPoints Calculation: 3.6

ZESTY LIME SHRIMP SKEWERS

Preparation Time: 15 min
Cooking Time: 10 min
Mode of Cooking: Grilling
Servings: 4
Ingredients:
- 1 lb peeled and deveined shrimp
- Juice and zest of 3 limes
- 1 Tbsp olive oil
- 1 tsp honey
- 1 clove garlic, minced
- 1 tsp ground cumin
- 1/2 tsp red pepper flakes
- Salt and black pepper to taste
- Fresh cilantro leaves, for garnish

Directions:
1. Combine lime juice, lime zest, olive oil, honey, garlic, cumin, and red pepper flakes in a bowl.
2. Add shrimp to the marinade and let sit for 10 minutes to absorb flavors.
3. Thread shrimp onto skewers.
4. Heat grill to medium-high.
5. Grill skewers for 2-3 minutes per side or until shrimp are opaque and cooked through.
6. Season with salt and black pepper, garnish with cilantro leaves.
7. Serve immediately.

Additional Tips:
- Replace honey with agave syrup for a vegan option.
- Pair with a side of grilled vegetables like bell peppers and zucchini for a complete meal.
- Use bamboo skewers soaked in water for at least 30 minutes prior to grilling to prevent burning.

Nutritional Values: Calories: 120 kcal, Protein: 23g, Fat: 3g, Saturated Fat: 0.5g, Carbohydrates: 4g, Sugars: 2g, Fiber: 1g, Sodium: 150mg

SmartPoints Calculation: 1.8

ROSEMARY-INFUSED MUSHROOM CAPS

Preparation Time: 15 min
Cooking Time: 20 min
Mode of Cooking: Baking
Servings: 4
Ingredients:
- 12 large mushroom caps, stems removed
- 2 Tbsp finely chopped fresh rosemary
- 3 cloves garlic, minced
- 1/4 cup finely diced red onion
- 1/4 cup crumbled feta cheese
- Olive oil spray
- Salt and black pepper to taste

Directions:
1. Preheat oven to 375°F (190°C).
2. Spray a baking sheet with olive oil spray.
3. In a bowl, mix rosemary, garlic, red onion, and feta cheese.
4. Stuff mixture into mushroom caps.
5. Place caps on the baking sheet.
6. Bake for 20 minutes or until mushrooms are tender.
7. Season with salt and black pepper.
8. Serve warm.

Additional Tips:
- Substitute feta with goat cheese for a creamier texture.
- Enhance flavor by drizzling with balsamic glaze before serving.
- Add crushed walnuts to the filling for added crunch and nutrition.

Nutritional Values: Calories: 90 kcal, Protein: 4g, Fat: 6g, Saturated Fat: 2g, Carbohydrates: 4g, Sugars: 2g, Fiber: 1g, Sodium: 180mg
SmartPoints Calculation: 3.1

9.2 SWEET TREATS WITHOUT THE GUILT

BAKED APPLES WITH CINNAMON

Preparation Time: 15 min
Cooking Time: 45 min
Mode of Cooking: Baking
Servings: 4
Ingredients:
- 4 large firm apples such as Granny Smith or Honeycrisp
- 4 tsp unsalted butter
- 4 Tbsp brown sugar substitute
- 1 tsp ground cinnamon
- 1/4 tsp ground nutmeg
- 1/4 cup chopped walnuts
- 1/2 cup water

Directions:
1. Core apples leaving the bottom intact, and peel the top third of each apple.
2. In a small bowl, mix together brown sugar substitute, cinnamon, nutmeg, and walnuts.
3. Fill each apple with this mixture and top each with a tsp of unsalted butter.
4. Place apples in a baking dish and add water to the bottom of the dish.
5. Bake in a preheated oven at 375°F (190°C) until apples are soft and the filling is bubbly, about 45 min.
6. Serve warm.

Additional Tips:
- Replace walnuts with pecans for a different texture and flavor.
- Serve with a dollop of non-fat Greek yogurt for extra creaminess without adding many calories.
- For extra spice, a pinch of clove can be added to the filling mixture.
- Baking time may vary based on the size and variety of the apples, so check for doneness by piercing them with a fork.

Nutritional Values: Calories: 150 kcal, Protein: 1g, Fat: 7g, Saturated Fat: 2g, Carbohydrates: 22g, Sugars: 16g, Fiber: 4g, Sodium: 50 mg
SmartPoints Calculation: 6.9

MIXED BERRY SORBET

Preparation Time: 120 min (including freezing)
Cooking Time: none
Mode of Cooking: Freezing
Servings: 6
Ingredients:
- 2 cups mixed berries (strawberries, blueberries, raspberries)
- 1/2 cup water
- 1/3 cup granulated sugar substitute
- 1 Tbsp fresh lemon juice

Directions:
1. Puree all berries in a blender until smooth.
2. In a medium saucepan over medium heat, combine water and sugar substitute, stirring until dissolved.
3. Combine berry puree and lemon juice with the sugar syrup in a bowl.
4. Freeze mixture in an ice cream maker according to manufacturer's instructions, then transfer to a freezer-safe container and freeze until firm, about 2 hr.

Additional Tips:
- Try different combinations of berries for varying tartness and sweetness.
- For a smoother texture, strain the berry mixture to remove seeds before freezing.
- Adding a few fresh mint leaves while blending can introduce a refreshing twist.
- No ice cream maker? Freeze the mixture in ice cube trays and blend cubes in a blender until smooth.

Nutritional Values: Calories: 70 kcal, Protein: 1g, Fat: 0g, Saturated Fat: 0g, Carbohydrates: 18g, Sugars: 12g, Fiber: 3g, Sodium: 5mg

SmartPoints Calculation: 3.5

FROZEN BANANA BITES WITH DARK CHOCOLATE DRIZZLE

Preparation Time: 60 min
Cooking Time: 2 min
Mode of Cooking: Freezing & Melting
Servings: 8
Ingredients:
- 4 large ripe bananas
- 1/2 cup dark chocolate chips
- 1 Tbsp coconut oil
- 1/4 cup crushed nuts (almonds, pistachios, or peanuts)

Directions:
1. Slice bananas into 1/2-inch thick rounds.
2. Arrange banana slices on a parchment-lined baking sheet and freeze until solid, about 1 hr.
3. Melt dark chocolate chips with coconut oil in a microwave or double boiler until smooth.
4. Drizzle melted chocolate over frozen banana slices and sprinkle with crushed nuts.
5. Freeze again until chocolate sets, about 15 min.

Additional Tips:
- Experiment with different toppings like shredded coconut or sea salt.
- Using a squeeze bottle for the chocolate drizzle can make the process cleaner and more controlled.
- Ensure bananas are not overly ripe to maintain firmness after freezing.

Nutritional Values: Calories: 100 kcal, Protein: 1.5g, Fat: 4.5g, Saturated Fat: 2g, Carbohydrates: 15g, Sugars: 10g, Fiber: 2g, Sodium: 0mg
SmartPoints Calculation: 4.7

CHILLED GRAPES WITH LIME ZEST

Preparation Time: 10 min
Cooking Time: none
Mode of Cooking: Chilling
Servings: 4
Ingredients:
- 2 lbs seedless grapes (green, red, or a mix)
- Zest of 1 lime
- 1 Tbsp fresh lime juice
- 1 tsp honey (optional)

Directions:
1. Wash grapes and remove from stems.
2. Toss grapes with lime zest, lime juice, and honey if using in a large bowl.
3. Chill in the refrigerator for at least 2 hr before serving.

Additional Tips:
- For a spicier twist, add a pinch of chili powder to the lime juice mixture.
- Mix in sliced peaches or melon for added variety and flavor.
- Serve chilled grapes as a refreshing side to spicy dishes or enjoy as a stand-alone snack.

Nutritional Values: Calories: 90 kcal, Protein: 1g, Fat: 0g, Saturated Fat: 0g, Carbohydrates: 23g, Sugars: 20g, Fiber: 1g, Sodium: 5mg
SmartPoints Calculation: 5

CHIA AND COCONUT YOGURT PARFAIT

Preparation Time: 15 mins
Cooking Time: none
Mode of Cooking: No Cooking
Servings: 2
Ingredients:
- 1 cup non-fat Greek yogurt
- 2 Tbsp chia seeds
- 1/2 cup mixed berries (strawberries, blueberries, raspberries)
- 2 Tbsp unsweetened coconut flakes
- 1/4 tsp pure vanilla extract

Directions:
1. Mix Ingredients: Combine non-fat Greek yogurt with chia seeds and vanilla extract in a bowl, stirring until well mixed.
2. Layer the Parfait: Start with a layer of the yogurt mixture at the bottom of two serving glasses, followed by a layer of mixed berries, and a sprinkle of coconut flakes. Repeat the layering until all ingredients are used up.

3. Chill: Refrigerate the parfaits for at least 10 minutes before serving to allow the chia seeds to swell and the flavors to meld.
4. Serve Chilled: Enjoy this refreshing parfait as a sweet treat without the guilt.

Additional Tips:
- Use Organic Berries: Opt for organic berries for a cleaner eat.
- Customize with Zero-Point Sweeteners: If you prefer a sweeter taste, add a zero-point sweetener like stevia or sucralose to the yogurt mix.
- Enhance Textures: Customize the texture by adding sugar-free muesli.
- Vitality Tip: Introduce a dash of cinnamon or nutmeg to boost both the flavor and metabolism-boosting properties of your parfait.

Nutritional Values: Calories: 180 kcal, Protein: 14g, Fat: 5g, Saturated Fat: 3g, Carbohydrates: 24g, Sugars: 8g, Fiber: 7g, Sodium: 85mg
SmartPoints Calculation: 5.9

SPICED PUMPKIN MOUSSE CUPS

Preparation Time: 10 mins
Cooking Time: none
Mode of Cooking: No Cooking
Servings: 4
Ingredients:
- 1 can (15 oz.) pure pumpkin puree
- 1 cup non-fat Greek yogurt
- 1/4 cup zero-point sweetener (erythritol)
- 1/2 tsp pumpkin pie spice
- 1/2 tsp cinnamon
- 1/4 tsp nutmeg

Directions:
1. Whip Together: In a large mixing bowl, combine pumpkin puree, non-fat Greek yogurt, zero-point sweetener, pumpkin pie spice, cinnamon, and nutmeg. Use an electric mixer to blend until the mixture becomes smooth and fluffy.
2. Serve: Distribute the mousse into four dessert cups. Garnish with a sprinkle of cinnamon if desired, and chill before serving.
3. Optional Chill: For best results, place the mousse cups in the refrigerator for at least one hour before serving to enhance the flavors.

Additional Tips:
- Pumpkin Puree Note: Ensure using 100% pure pumpkin puree, not pumpkin pie filling, which contains added sugars and syrups.
- Winter Spice Variation: You can adjust the level of spices according to taste preference or add a pinch of clove for an extra kick.
- Garnishing Options: Top with a dollop of whipped zero-point cream for an indulgent yet guilt-free presentation.

Nutritional Values: Calories: 90 kcal, Protein: 6g, Fat: 0.5g, Saturated Fat: 0g, Carbohydrates: 15g, Sugars: 4g, Fiber: 4g, Sodium: 40mg
SmartPoints Calculation: 2.6

PEAR AND RICOTTA SPICE BOATS

Preparation Time: 20 mins
Cooking Time: none
Mode of Cooking: No Cooking
Servings: 6
Ingredients:
- 3 large pears
- 1 cup non-fat ricotta cheese
- 1 tsp cinnamon
- 1/4 tsp allspice
- 2 Tbsp chopped walnuts
- 1 Tbsp honey (optional)
- Fresh mint leaves for garnish

Directions:
1. Prepare Pears: Halve the pears and carefully scoop out the cores to create a 'boat' for the filling.
2. Mix Filling: In a bowl, combine non-fat ricotta cheese, cinnamon, allspice, and honey if using. Mix until well combined.
3. Fill and Garnish: Spoon the ricotta mixture into the pear halves. Sprinkle chopped walnuts on top and garnish with fresh mint leaves.

4. Serve Immediately: Serve these flavorful boats immediately, or chill briefly to meld the flavors.

Additional Tips:
- Seasonal Pears: Use ripe but firm pears for the best texture and sweetness.
- Nut Variations: Substitute walnuts with pecans or almonds for different textures and flavors.
- Honey Optional: Eliminate honey for a lower sugar option, or replace it with a zero-point sweetener to maintain sweetness.

Nutritional Values: Calories: 150 kcal, Protein: 8g, Fat: 5g, Saturated Fat: 0.5g, Carbohydrates: 22g, Sugars: 16g, Fiber: 4g, Sodium: 60mg
SmartPoints Calculation: 5.8

ZESTY LEMON FROYO BITES

Preparation Time: 15 mins
Cooking Time: 2 hrs (Freezing Time)
Mode of Cooking: Freezing
Servings: 8
Ingredients:
- 2 cups non-fat Greek yogurt
- Zest of 1 lemon
- 1/4 cup fresh lemon juice
- 3 Tbsp zero-point sweetener (erythritol)
- Fresh raspberries for topping

Directions:
1. Mix In a bowl, combine non-fat Greek yogurt, lemon zest, lemon juice, and zero-point sweetener until smooth.
2. Prepare Molds: Pour the yogurt mixture into silicone ice cube molds or small cupcake liners. Top each mold with a raspberry.
3. Freeze: Place the molds in the freezer and allow to set for at least 2 hours, or until fully frozen.
4. Serve Frozen: Once set, pop the FroYo bites out of the molds and serve immediately for a refreshing, tangy treat.

Additional Tips:
- Lemon Freshness: Use freshly squeezed lemon juice for the best flavor.
- Mold Choices: Use different shaped silicone molds for a fun variety of shapes.
- Serving Suggestion: Serve these bites after a light meal for a refreshing end to your dining experience.

Nutritional Values: Calories: 45 kcal, Protein: 6g, Fat: 0g, Saturated Fat: 0g, Carbohydrates: 6g, Sugars: 4g, Fiber: 0g, Sodium: 20mg
SmartPoints Calculation: 1.3

CHAI SPICED POACHED PEARS

Preparation Time: 10 min
Cooking Time: 25 min
Mode of Cooking: Poaching
Servings: 4
Ingredients:
- 4 ripe but firm pears, peeled and cored
- 4 cups of water
- 3 Tbsp honey
- 2 cinnamon sticks
- 6 whole cloves
- 1 star anise
- 2 black tea bags
- 1 tsp vanilla extract
- zest of 1 orange

Directions:
1. Prepare the poaching liquid: In a large saucepan, combine water, honey, cinnamon sticks, cloves, star anise, and orange zest. Bring to a simmer.
2. Add the pears: Once the liquid is simmering, add the pears and tea bags. Reduce the heat and let simmer gently for 25 minutes, or until the pears are tender.
3. Cool and serve: Remove the pears from the liquid and let them cool. Reduce the poaching liquid by continuing to simmer until thickened, about 10 minutes. Stir in vanilla extract. Serve the pears with a drizzle of the reduced poaching liquid.

Additional Tips:
- Use Green Tea for a Milder Flavor: If black tea feels too strong, green tea can be a softer alternative.

- **Poach in Advance:** These pears can be poached in advance and stored in their liquid in the refrigerator, absorbing more flavors as they sit.
- **Serving Suggestion:** Serve with a dollop of fat-free Greek yogurt for added creaminess without guilt.

Nutritional Values: Calories: 120 kcal, Protein: 0.5g, Fat: 0.3g, Saturated Fat: 0g, Carbohydrates: 31g, Sugars: 20g, Fiber: 5g, Sodium: 2mg
SmartPoints Calculation: 6

ZESTY LIME YOGURT FREEZE

Preparation Time: 15 min
Cooking Time: 2 hr (freezing time)
Mode of Cooking: Freezing
Servings: 6
Ingredients:
- 3 cups non-fat Greek yogurt
- zest of 3 limes
- juice of 3 limes
- 1 Tbsp honey

Directions:
1. Combine Ingredients: In a mixing bowl, whisk together the Greek yogurt, lime zest, lime juice, and honey until well blended.
2. Freeze: Pour the mixture into an ice cube tray or a shallow baking dish and freeze for about 2 hours or until firm.
3. Serve: Once frozen, break into chunks or use a fork to scrape into fluffy crystals. Serve immediately.

Additional Tips:
- **Make it Minty:** Add fresh chopped mint for a refreshing twist.
- **Sweetness Adjustment:** Adjust honey according to your taste or substitute with agave syrup for a different kind of sweetness.
- **Optimal Serving:** Serve immediately after scraping for the best texture, akin to a granita.

Nutritional Values: Calories: 90 kcal, Protein: 12g, Fat: 0g, Saturated Fat: 0g, Carbohydrates: 10g, Sugars: 8g, Fiber: 0g, Sodium: 30mg
SmartPoints Calculation: 2.5

9.3 HEALTHY PARTY PLATTERS AND APPETIZERS

GRILLED ZUCCHINI ROLL-UPS WITH HERBED GOAT CHEESE AND PEPPERS

Preparation Time: 15 min
Cooking Time: 10 min
Mode of Cooking: Grilling
Servings: 8
Ingredients:
- 3 medium zucchinis, thinly sliced lengthwise
- 4 oz herbed goat cheese
- 1 red bell pepper, julienned
- 1 yellow bell pepper, julienned
- 1 Tbsp olive oil
- Fresh herbs (such as basil or parsley), for garnish
- Salt and black pepper to taste

Directions:
1. Slice the Zucchini: Using a mandoline or sharp knife, slice the zucchinis lengthwise into thin strips. Brush each strip lightly with olive oil and season with salt and pepper.
2. Grill the Zucchini: Preheat grill to medium-high heat (about 375°F (190°C)). Grill zucchini strips for 2-3 min on each side, or until tender and grill marks appear. Remove and let cool slightly.
3. Prepare the Filling: Spread herbed goat cheese evenly along one side of each grilled zucchini strip. Top with julienned red and yellow bell peppers.
4. Roll Them Up: Roll up the zucchini strips tightly from one end to the other. Garnish with fresh herbs before serving.

Additional Tips:
- **Use a Vegetable Grill Basket:** For easier grilling, use a vegetable grill basket to prevent the zucchini from falling through the grates.
- **Herbed Goat Cheese Substitution:** If herbed goat cheese is unavailable, mix plain goat cheese with finely chopped herbs of your choice.

- Serve as a Side or Appetizer: These roll-ups are perfect as a side dish or can be served as an elegant appetizer for gatherings.

Nutritional Values: Calories: 90 kcal, Protein: 5g, Fat: 7g, Saturated Fat: 3g, Carbohydrates: 3g, Sugars: 2g, Fiber: 1g, Sodium: 80mg

SmartPoints Calculation: 3.3

SPICED CAULIFLOWER BITES WITH CILANTRO YOGURT DIP

Preparation Time: 20 min
Cooking Time: 25 min
Mode of Cooking: Baking
Servings: 6
Ingredients:
- 1 large head of cauliflower, broken into florets
- 2 Tbsp olive oil
- 1 Tbsp curry powder
- 1 tsp smoked paprika
- 1/2 tsp garlic powder
- Salt and black pepper to taste
- 1 cup non-fat Greek yogurt
- 2 Tbsp chopped fresh cilantro
- 1 Tbsp lime juice
- 1 clove garlic, minced

Directions:
1. Prep the Cauliflower: Preheat oven to 425°F (220°C). In a large bowl, toss cauliflower florets with olive oil, curry powder, smoked paprika, garlic powder, salt, and pepper until well coated.
2. Bake the Cauliflower: Spread the florets on a baking sheet in a single layer. Bake for 25 min or until crispy and golden.
3. Make the Dip: While the cauliflower is baking, combine Greek yogurt, chopped cilantro, lime juice, and minced garlic in a small bowl. Chill until ready to serve.
4. Serve: Arrange the baked cauliflower bites on a platter and serve with the cilantro yogurt dip side by side.

Additional Tips:
- Cauliflower Florets: Ensure florets are small and uniform for even cooking.
- Smoking Paprika Alternative: For a milder flavor, substitute smoked paprika with regular paprika.
- Greek Yogurt: Ensure you use non-fat Greek yogurt to keep the recipe within WW guidelines.

Nutritional Values: Calories: 70 kcal, Protein: 4g, Fat: 3.5g, Saturated Fat: 0.5g, Carbohydrates: 8g, Sugars: 4g, Fiber: 3g, Sodium: 55mg

SmartPoints Calculation: 2.4

CHERRY TOMATO AND MOZZARELLA PESTO SKEWERS

Preparation Time: 10 min
Cooking Time: none
Mode of Cooking: No Cooking
Servings: 10
Ingredients:
- 20 cherry tomatoes
- 10 small fresh mozzarella balls
- 10 fresh basil leaves
- 2 Tbsp pesto sauce
- 10 wooden skewers
- Salt and black pepper to taste

Directions:
1. Assemble the Skewers: Thread a cherry tomato, a basil leaf, and a mozzarella ball onto each skewer. Repeat until all ingredients are used up.
2. Season and Serve: Drizzle pesto sauce over the assembled skewers. Season with salt and black pepper to taste. Serve immediately or cover and refrigerate until serving.

Additional Tips:
- Variety of Tomatoes: Use a mix of red and yellow cherry tomatoes for a vibrant display.
- Basil Substitute: If basil is not available, use spinach or arugula for a peppery kick.
- Pesto Variations: Use sun-dried tomato pesto for a twist on the traditional green basil pesto.

Nutritional Values: Calories: 70 kcal, Protein: 5g, Fat: 5g, Saturated Fat: 2g, Carbohydrates: 2g, Sugars: 1g, Fiber: 0.5g, Sodium: 200mg
SmartPoints Calculation: 2.3

SMOKED SALMON CUCUMBER CUPS

Preparation Time: 15 min
Cooking Time: none
Mode of Cooking: No Cooking
Servings: 12
Ingredients:

- 2 large English cucumbers
- 8 oz smoked salmon, finely chopped
- 1/4 cup non-fat Greek yogurt
- 1 Tbsp capers, finely chopped
- 1 Tbsp dill, finely chopped
- 1 tsp lemon zest
- Salt and black pepper to taste

Directions:

1. Prepare the Cucumbers: Cut the cucumbers into 1-inch thick rounds. Using a melon baller or small spoon, scoop out the centers to create cups.
2. Mix the Filling: In a bowl, combine smoked salmon, Greek yogurt, capers, dill, and lemon zest. Season with salt and black pepper. Mix until well combined.
3. Fill and Serve: Spoon the salmon mixture into the cucumber cups. Arrange on a platter and serve chilled.

Additional Tips:

- Cucumber Selection: Choose firm, medium-sized English cucumbers for best results.
- Serving Option: These cucumber cups can be topped with a small sprig of dill or a caper for added visual appeal.
- Make Ahead: Prepare the salmon mixture a day in advance and fill the cucumber cups just before serving to save time.

Nutritional Values: Calories: 50 kcal, Protein: 6g, Fat: 2g, Saturated Fat: 0g, Carbohydrates: 1g, Sugars: 1g, Fiber: 0g, Sodium: 200mg
SmartPoints Calculation: 1.1

MINI MEDITERRANEAN FRITTATA MUFFINS

Preparation Time: 15 min
Cooking Time: 25 min
Mode of Cooking: Baking
Servings: 12
Ingredients:

- 8 eggs
- 1 cup chopped spinach
- 1/2 cup diced tomatoes
- 1/4 cup crumbled feta cheese
- 1/4 cup finely chopped onions
- 1/2 cup skim milk
- 1 tsp olive oil
- 1/2 tsp salt
- 1/4 tsp black pepper

Directions:

1. Prepare Oven and Muffin Tin: Preheat oven to 375°F (190°C). Lightly grease a 12-cup muffin tin with olive oil.
2. Combine Ingredients: In a large bowl, whisk together eggs, skim milk, salt, and pepper. Add in spinach, tomatoes, onions, and feta cheese, mixing until evenly distributed.
3. Fill Muffin Cups: Evenly divide the egg mixture among the prepared muffin cups, filling each about 2/3 full.
4. Bake Muffins: Place the muffin tin in the oven and bake for 20-25 minutes, or until the eggs are fully set and the tops are slightly golden.
5. Serve Warm: Allow to cool for a few minutes before removing from the tin. Serve warm or store in an airtight container for later use.

Additional Tips:

- Make Ahead Option: These muffins can be made in advance and stored in the refrigerator for a quick, protein-packed snack or breakfast on the go.
- Customizable Ingredients: Feel free to swap out vegetables depending on preference or what you have on hand. Bell peppers or zucchini make great alternatives.

Nutritional Values: Calories: 90 kcal, Protein: 7g, Fat: 6g, Saturated Fat: 2g, Carbohydrates: 2g, Sugars: 1g, Fiber: 0.5g, Sodium: 230mg
SmartPoints Calculation: 2.7

ROASTED RED PEPPER AND ARTICHOKE TAPENADE

Preparation Time: 10 min
Cooking Time: none
Mode of Cooking: No Cooking
Servings: 8
Ingredients:
- 1 jar (12 oz) roasted red peppers, drained and chopped
- 1 can (6 oz) artichoke hearts, drained and chopped
- 1/4 cup chopped fresh parsley
- 2 Tbsp capers, drained
- 2 Tbsp lemon juice
- 1 Tbsp olive oil
- 1 clove garlic, minced
- Salt and black pepper to taste

Directions:
1. Combine Ingredients: In a food processor, combine roasted red peppers, artichoke hearts, parsley, capers, lemon juice, olive oil, and garlic. Blend until the mixture is coarsely chopped but not pureed.
2. Season Tapenade: Taste and season with salt and pepper as needed.
3. Chill Before Serving: Transfer the tapenade to a bowl, cover, and chill for at least 30 minutes to allow flavors to meld.
4. Serve with Veggie Crisps: Serve chilled with zero-point vegetable crisps or spread on a WW-friendly cracker for a fulfilling snack.

Additional Tips:
- Serving Tip: Garnish with extra chopped parsley for a fresh, herbal hit just before serving.
- Make Ahead: This tapenade can be made a day ahead and stored in the refrigerator to enhance its flavors.

Nutritional Values: Calories: 70 kcal, Protein: 1g, Fat: 4.5g, Saturated Fat: 0.5g, Carbohydrates: 7g, Sugars: 2g, Fiber: 2g, Sodium: 340mg
SmartPoints Calculation: 2.4

CHILLED GINGER PEACH SOUP

Preparation Time: 15 min
Cooking Time: none
Mode of Cooking: No Cooking
Servings: 4
Ingredients:
- 4 large peaches, peeled and diced
- 2 Tbsp grated fresh ginger
- 1 cup non-fat Greek yogurt
- 1 Tbsp honey
- Juice of 1 lemon
- Mint leaves for garnish

Directions:
1. Prepare Ingredients: Combine peaches, grated ginger, Greek yogurt, honey, and lemon juice in a blender.
2. Blend Until Smooth: Blend until the mixture is smooth.
3. Chill Thoroughly: Pour the soup into a large bowl, cover, and refrigerate for at least 1 hr to chill and develop the flavors.
4. Serve Chilled: Serve the soup chilled, garnished with fresh mint leaves for an extra touch of freshness.

Additional Tips:
- Use Ripe Peaches: For a sweeter soup, ensure the peaches are very ripe.
- Ginger Adjustment: Adjust the amount of ginger according to your taste preference, more for a spicier kick, less for a milder version.
- Serving Idea: For an elegant presentation, serve in chilled bowls or cups with a spoonful of additional Greek yogurt swirled on top.

Nutritional Values: Calories: 110 kcal, Protein: 4g, Fat: 0.5g, Saturated Fat: 0g, Carbohydrates: 22g, Sugars: 20g, Fiber: 2g, Sodium: 20mg
SmartPoints Calculation: 5.4

ZESTY LIME GRILLED SHRIMP SKEWERS

Preparation Time: 15 min
Cooking Time: 10 min
Mode of Cooking: Grilling
Servings: 4
Ingredients:
- 12 large shrimp, peeled and deveined
- 1 Tbsp olive oil
- Juice and zest of 1 lime
- 1 tsp chili powder
- 1/2 tsp garlic powder
- 1/4 tsp salt
- Fresh cilantro for garnish
- Lime wedges for serving

Directions:
1. Prepare the shrimp: In a mixing bowl, combine olive oil, lime juice and zest, chili powder, garlic powder, and salt. Add shrimp and toss to coat evenly. Allow to marinate for 10 minutes.
2. Preheat grill to medium-high heat (around 375°F (190°C)). Thread shrimp onto skewers.
3. Grill the shrimp skewers: Place skewers on the grill. Cook for about 5 minutes on each side, or until shrimp are pink and opaque.
4. Serve: Garnish with fresh cilantro and serve with lime wedges on the side.

Additional Tips:
- Use skewers made of bamboo: Soak them in water for at least 30 min before grilling to avoid burning.
- Enhance flavor: Add a pinch of cumin to the marinade for a smoky twist.

Nutritional Values: Calories: 120 kcal, Protein: 18g, Fat: 5g, Saturated Fat: 0.5g, Carbohydrates: 3g, Sugars: 0g, Fiber: 0g, Sodium: 200mg
SmartPoints Calculation: 2

CREAMY BABA GANOUSH WITH POMEGRANATE

Preparation Time: 15 min
Cooking Time: 45 min
Mode of Cooking: Baking
Servings: 6
Ingredients:
- 2 large eggplants
- 2 Tbsp tahini
- 1 Tbsp lemon juice
- 2 cloves garlic, minced
- 1/4 tsp smoked paprika
- Salt to taste
- 2 Tbsp pomegranate seeds
- 1 Tbsp chopped parsley

Directions:
1. Roast the eggplants: Preheat oven to 400°F (200°C). Prick eggplants with a fork and place on a baking sheet. Bake until soft and collapsed, about 45 min.
2. Prepare the dip: Scoop out the eggplant flesh into a food processor. Add tahini, lemon juice, garlic, and smoked paprika. Process until smooth. Season with salt.
3. Serve: Transfer to a serving bowl, sprinkle with pomegranate seeds and chopped parsley.

Additional Tips:
- Enhance smokiness: Char the eggplants on the grill before baking for a richer flavor.
- Extra creamy texture: Add 1 Tbsp of Greek yogurt to the food processor.
- Decorative touch: Drizzle with olive oil and sprinkle additional smoked paprika before serving.

Nutritional Values: Calories: 80 kcal, Protein: 2g, Fat: 3g, Saturated Fat: 0g, Carbohydrates: 13g, Sugars: 6g, Fiber: 6g, Sodium: 40mg
SmartPoints Calculation: 3

SAVORY MUSHROOM MINI TARTS

Preparation Time: 20 min
Cooking Time: 25 min
Mode of Cooking: Baking
Servings: 12
Ingredients:
- 12 mini tart shells
- 1 Tbsp extra virgin olive oil
- 1/2 lb mixed mushrooms, finely chopped
- 1 small onion, minced
- 1 clove garlic, minced

- 1 tsp thyme leaves
- 2 Tbsp white wine
- Salt and pepper to taste
- 1/4 cup grated Parmesan cheese
- Fresh thyme for garnish

Directions:

1. Prepare the filling: Heat olive oil in a skillet over medium heat. Add mushrooms, onion, and garlic, sauté until softened, about 8 min. Add thyme and white wine, cook until liquid is absorbed. Season with salt and pepper.
2. Fill the tarts: Spoon the mushroom mixture into mini tart shells. Top each with a sprinkle of Parmesan cheese.
3. Bake the tarts: Preheat oven to 375°F (190°C). Bake the filled tart shells for about 15 min, or until the edges are golden brown.
4. Serve: Garnish with fresh thyme.

Additional Tips:

- Use various mushrooms: Incorporate shiitake, cremini, or portobello for depth of flavor.
- Make-ahead strategy: Prepare the mushroom mixture in advance and refrigerate overnight.
- Vegan option: Substitute Parmesan with nutritional yeast for a cheese-like flavor.

Nutritional Values: Calories: 150 kcal, Protein: 4g, Fat: 10g, Saturated Fat: 3g, Carbohydrates: 12g, Sugars: 2g, Fiber: 1g, Sodium: 115mg

SmartPoints Calculation: 5.2

CHAPTER 10: FOUR-WEEK MEAL PLAN

Welcome to the heart of transformation—the four-week meal plan that promises not just to change how you eat, but also how you feel, live, and engage with your world. Over the next thirty days, you're not just following recipes; you're embarking on a culinary journey designed to infuse your body with vitality and your life with newfound rhythm and ease.

Imagine this: each day begins not with the frantic scramble we've all known too well, but with serene confidence. You'll find solace in knowing exactly what's on your menu, each meal perfectly balanced to align with your weight loss and health goals. Picture the peace of mind that comes with having your entire week's meals planned out — freeing up precious time to truly live, laugh, and cherish the moments that matter most with family and friends.

Throughout this chapter, we dive deep into an ensemble of dishes that celebrate flavor without complicating your schedule. From the zesty tang of a lemon-garlic roasted chicken to the comforting embrace of a rich, herb-infused soup, these recipes are curated not only to satisfy your taste buds but also to ensure that you stay on track with your wellness journey, effortlessly and joyously.

You'll discover meals that are as quick as they are beneficial, crafted for cooks of all levels, ensuring no one is left behind due to complexity or obscure ingredients. This plan is more than a simple guide—it's a companion on your journey to a healthier lifestyle, where the energy you gain from these meals propels you through even the busiest of days.

As we progress through these four weeks together, remember that each dish is an essential building block in your life's new structure. It's not just about losing weight; it's about gaining a lifestyle where balance, health, and pleasure coexist. Let's embrace this delectable adventure with open arms and a hearty appetite, one day, one meal, one savory bite at a time.

10.1 WEEK 1: JUMPSTART YOUR JOURNEY

WEEK 1	breakfast	snack	lunch	snack	dinner
Monday	Berry Almond Breakfast Quinoa	Spiced Turmeric Roasted Chickpeas	Grilled Peach and Chicken Salad	Savory Egg & Sea Salt Snackers	Zesty Lemon Dill Baked Salmon
Tuesday	Chia Seed Pudding with Fresh Berries	Cool Cucumber Yogurt Bites	Herbed Lemon Shrimp and Asparagus	Roasted Red Pepper and Artichoke Tapenade	Colorful Shrimp Stir-Fry with Broccoli and Peppers
Wednesday	Zesty Tofu and Spinach Scramble Bowl	Savory Egg & Sea Salt Snackers	Zesty Lime Shrimp and Avocado Salad	Mini Mediterranean Frittata Muffins	Herbed Turkey Meatballs with Marinara Sauce
Thursday	Smoked Salmon and Avocado Bowl	Roasted Red Pepper and Artichoke Tapenade	Crispy Tofu and Kale Salad with Tahini Dressing	Green Tea Mint Medley Smoothie	Zesty Lime & Herb Turkey Quinoa Bowl
Friday	Sunny Mediterranean Breakfast Bowl	Mini Mediterranean Frittata Muffins	Beetroot and Goat Cheese Salad with Walnuts	Spicy Tomato and White Bean Toast	Savory Spinach & Mushroom Stuffed Bell Peppers
Saturday	Greek Yogurt and Fruit Parfait Bowl	Green Tea Mint Medley Smoothie	Tangy Citrus Fennel Salad	Overnight Oats with Almond Butter and Banana	Herb-Infused Chicken and Root Vegetable Roast
Sunday	Oatmeal with Cinnamon and Sliced Apples	Spicy Tomato and White Bean Toast	Asian Slaw with Peanut Dressing	Veggie-Packed Egg Muffins	Garlic Lemon Baked Tilapia

10.2 WEEK 2: BUILDING MOMENTUM

WEEK 2	breakfast	snack	lunch	snack	dinner
Monday	Sunrise Salmon and Avocado Bowl	Overnight Oats with Almond Butter and Banana	Mediterranean Chickpea Salad	Whole Grain Toast with Avocado and Tomato	Zesty Lemon Basil Tilapia
Tuesday	Mushroom and Spinach Frittata Cups	Veggie-Packed Egg Muffins	Spicy Watermelon and Cucumber Gazpacho	Cottage Cheese with Pineapple Chunks	Spiced Chickpea Stuffed Bell Peppers
Wednesday	Overnight Oats with Almond Butter and Banana	Whole Grain Toast with Avocado and Tomato	Roasted Beet and Goat Cheese Salad	Zesty Ginger-Peach Yogurt Parfait	Grilled Chicken Breast with Asparagus
Thursday	Veggie-Packed Egg Muffins	Cottage Cheese with Pineapple Chunks	Asian Sesame Edamame Salad	Savory Spinach and Mushroom Egg White Cups	Stuffed Bell Peppers with Quinoa and Vegetables
Friday	Whole Grain Toast with Avocado and Tomato	Zesty Ginger-Peach Yogurt Parfait	Turkey and Avocado Lettuce Wrap	Warm Cinnamon Apple Quinoa Bowl	Roasted Cauliflower Steaks with Chimichurri Sauce
Saturday	Cottage Cheese with Pineapple Chunks	Savory Spinach and Mushroom Egg White Cups	Spicy Tomato and Red Lentil Soup	Quinoa and Berry Breakfast Bowl	Spaghetti Squash with Tomato Basil Sauce
Sunday	Zesty Ginger-Peach Yogurt Parfait	Warm Cinnamon Apple Quinoa Bowl	Miso Umami Soup	Smoked Salmon and Avocado Bowl	Grilled Portobello Mushrooms with Balsamic Glaze

10.3 Week 3: Maintaining Balance

WEEK 3	breakfast	snack	lunch	snack	dinner
Monday	Savory Spinach and Mushroom Egg White Cups	Quinoa and Berry Breakfast Bowl	Creamy Roasted Cauliflower Soup	Sunny Mediterranean Breakfast Bowl	Spiced Cauliflower and Chickpea Stew
Tuesday	Warm Cinnamon Apple Quinoa Bowl	Smoked Salmon and Avocado Bowl	Chicken and Vegetable Soup	Greek Yogurt and Fruit Parfait Bowl	Sesame Ginger Tofu Stir-Fry
Wednesday	Quinoa and Berry Breakfast Bowl	Sunny Mediterranean Breakfast Bowl	Butternut Squash and Carrot Soup	Oatmeal with Cinnamon and Sliced Apples	Baked Spinach and Artichoke Hearts
Thursday	Mini Mediterranean Frittata Muffins	Greek Yogurt and Fruit Parfait Bowl	Tomato Basil Soup with Grilled Shrimp	Sunrise Salmon and Avocado Bowl	Roasted Eggplant with Tomato Relish
Friday	Savory Egg & Sea Salt Snackers	Oatmeal with Cinnamon and Sliced Apples	Lentil and Spinach Soup	Mushroom and Spinach Frittata Cups	Savory Spinach and Artichoke Galettes
Saturday	Cool Cucumber Yogurt Bites	Sunrise Salmon and Avocado Bowl	Saffron Infused Cauliflower Soup	Cool Cucumber Yogurt Bites	Curried Cauliflower with Lentils
Sunday	Smoked Salmon and Cucumber Nori Rolls	Mushroom and Spinach Frittata Cups	Miso Mushroom Broth	Savory Egg & Sea Salt Snackers	One-Pot Chicken and Quinoa with Spinach

10.4 Week 4: Sustaining Success

WEEK 4	breakfast	snack	lunch	snack	dinner
Monday	Grilled Chicken and Veggie Wrap with Hummus	Cool Cucumber Yogurt Bites	Lemon Pepper Veggie Soup	Roasted Red Pepper and Artichoke Tapenade	Sheet Pan Baked Cod with Vegetables
Tuesday	Tuna Salad Lettuce Wrap with Pickles	Savory Egg & Sea Salt Snackers	Smoked Salmon and Cucumber Nori Rolls	Mini Mediterranean Frittata Muffins	One-Pot Turkey Chili with Beans
Wednesday	Egg Salad Sandwich with Whole Grain Bread	Roasted Red Pepper and Artichoke Tapenade	Spicy Grilled Veggie & Hummus Wrap	Green Tea Mint Medley Smoothie	Roasted Salmon and Fennel with Citrus Herb Sauce
Thursday	Zesty Lemon-Pepper Tofu Wrap	Mini Mediterranean Frittata Muffins	Chimichurri Chickpea Salad Wrap	Spiced Turmeric Roasted Chickpeas	Spicy Paprika and Garlic Shrimp
Friday	Spicy Chickpea and Spinach Wrap	Green Tea Mint Medley Smoothie	Grilled Chicken and Veggie Wrap with Hummus	Cool Cucumber Yogurt Bites	Lemon Thyme Chicken
Saturday	Grilled Vegetable and Goat Cheese Burrito	Spiced Turmeric Roasted Chickpeas	Grilled Peach and Chicken Salad	Savory Egg & Sea Salt Snackers	Mediterranean Vegetable and Chickpea Stew
Sunday	Berry Almond Breakfast Quinoa	Cool Cucumber Yogurt Bites	Herbed Lemon Shrimp and Asparagus	Roasted Red Pepper and Artichoke Tapenade	Zesty Lemon Dill Baked Salmon

Chapter 11: Tips and Tricks for Long-Term Success

Embarking on a journey toward wellness and weight loss is akin to setting sail across a vast ocean. The waters of diet and healthy living, while promising, are dotted with challenges that can make the route seem daunting. However, with the right set of navigation tools, the journey can not only become manageable but also enjoyable. Through previous chapters, we've charted the course by exploring flavorful recipes and simple strategies to incorporate into your daily routine. As we venture into the realm of long-term success, it's essential to embrace not just a series of dietary changes but a transformation in lifestyle that endures.

Imagine, if you will, the joy of reaching that moment where balance becomes second nature. Where making healthy choices doesn't feel like a chore, but rather a fulfilling part of your everyday life. It's here, in Chapter 11, that we'll unpack the secrets to maintaining this equilibrium. These are not just tips, but life lessons that transform temporary success into a lasting legacy of health and vigor.

Consider Laura, a dedicated nurse and mother of two, who found herself struggling to juggle her career, family life, and personal health. Her turning point came when she realized it wasn't about drastic diets or temporary fixes, but about building a foundation of habits that could support her busy lifestyle indefinitely. We'll delve into stories like Laura's, tapping into the real-world experiences of individuals who have navigated their paths - the setbacks and victories that define a sustainable approach to weight loss.

This chapter is your guide to embedding resilience and adaptability into your wellness strategy. We'll explore how to harmonize your goals with life's unpredictable rhythms, ensuring that your dietary habits can flex and evolve with your changing circumstances. Here, the focus is on not just achieving, but maintaining your wellness milestones.

By the end of this discussion, you'll have a toolkit that is not merely about managing weight, but about celebrating life - a life where health is interwoven into the fabric of your daily existence, not at odds with it. Let's step confidently into this chapter, ready to embrace the techniques that will anchor your long-term wellness journey.

11.1 Adapting the Plan to Your Lifestyle

Our diet plans, much like our lives, are deeply personal and influenced by the unique rhythms of our day-to-day activities. One of the core principles of sustained weight loss is adapting dietary approaches to fit personal lifestyle choices, rather than trying to mold your life around a rigid, one-size-fits-all plan. This dynamic, flexible approach enables you to maintain your weight loss journey over the long haul, turning good practices into habitual elements of your routine.

Ask yourself, "How can I integrate healthy eating into my daily life seamlessly?" Consider Tom, a single father and a software developer, who initially struggled to balance his hectic schedule with cooking healthy meals. Rather than surrendering to convenience foods, he learned to prep meals on Sundays, ensuring he had healthy, reusable components like grilled chicken, roasted vegetables, and cooked grains ready to go. This shift didn't just change Tom's eating habits; it transformed his approach to meal planning, making it a pivotal element of his week, adaptable to his fluctuating work and personal commitments.

Take Sarah, a college student juggling studies and a part-time job. Her challenge was not just managing time but also budget constraints. She started focusing on versatile, nutrient-rich, and affordable staples like beans, rice, and seasonal vegetables. Sarah's story illustrates that modifying your food choices based on financial and time resources can still align with your health and weight goals.

Flexibility goes beyond just ingredients or meal timing. It involves understanding the deeper relationship between your eating habits and your daily life dynamics. For instance, if you're someone with a fluctuating schedule, like a nurse or a police officer, you might benefit from learning the art of 'smart snacking'. This could mean having a stash of nuts, yogurt, or fruit at work, which can help in preventing hunger pangs and avoiding the vending machine trap.

Moreover, adapting your plan needs a mindset shift. It's not enough to make changes; it's crucial to cultivate a positive attitude towards these changes. Consider how these adjustments not only benefit your diet but how they can positively impact other areas of your life. For instance, by integrating more physical activity into your routine, you not only aid your weight loss efforts but also enhance your mood and energy levels, making everyday tasks feel more manageable and enjoyable.

Dining out, a common challenge for many, doesn't have to derail your diet plan. When eating at restaurants, it's about smart choices. Opt for dishes that are grilled, baked, or steamed, and don't hesitate to request modifications that suit your dietary needs. Remember, most chefs and eateries are more than willing to accommodate such requests. It's about communicating your needs clearly and assertively.

Let's not overlook the social aspect of eating. Social gatherings often center around food, and it can be challenging to stick to your diet when faced with tempting dishes. Here, it's strategic to eat a healthy snack before attending events to avoid overindulgence. Also, focus on the social interaction rather than the eating itself; remember, you're there to connect with people, not just to eat.

An important aspect of any adaptable plan is continual assessment and adjustment. What worked for you at the beginning of your weight loss journey may not be as effective as you progress. Regularly taking stock of your progress and making necessary tweaks is crucial. Maybe you've hit a plateau, or life has thrown you a curveball that necessitates a shift in your routine. Stay agile, be open to testing new strategies, and most importantly, stay committed to the journey.

Understanding that setbacks are part of the process is also vital. Each setback is a learning opportunity, not a failure. If you find yourself slipping back into old habits, take a moment to assess what led to that slip. Was it stress, a disruption in routine, or perhaps feeling unprepared? Use this insight to fortify your plan against future disruptions.

Lastly, remember the importance of support. Whether it's friends, family, or a community group, having people who support your goals and understand the importance of your journey can make a significant difference. They can help hold you accountable, offer encouragement during challenging times, and celebrate your successes with you.

In conclusion, adapting your dietary plan to fit your lifestyle is not just about making temporary changes; it's about transforming your approach to food, understanding its role in your life, and ensuring that your eating habits evolve along with your circumstances. By staying flexible, proactive, and positive, you make your weight loss journey not just about reaching a number on a scale, but about leading a healthier, fuller life. Embrace the changes, enjoy the process, and let your diet plan be a living, breathing part of your world, adaptable and responsive to your life's needs.

11.2 STAYING INSPIRED AND INFORMED

The path to maintaining long-term weight loss success is as much about keeping your mind engaged and your heart inspired as it is about managing what you eat. Staying informed and inspired can transform the weight loss journey from a fleeting endeavor into a vibrant lifestyle transformation. This involves continually refreshing your ideas, knowledge, and motivational sources to nurture both mental and emotional well-being.

Picture Mark, whose initial enthusiasm for a healthier lifestyle began to wane after a few months. What revived his motivation was not a drastic diet change, but reconnecting with why he started: to be an active participant in his children's lives. He began subscribing to health blogs, listening to podcasts on nutrition, and joining online communities. These resources not only kept him informed about health trends but also connected him with stories of people on similar journeys, reigniting his motivation.

At the heart of staying inspired is the power of personal storytelling. Engagement with the stories of others who are navigating the same path can provide a sense of community and shared struggle. Whether it is through books, articles, or shared experiences in group sessions, hearing about how others overcome their challenges can propel you through moments of doubt.

In addition to personal narratives, maintaining an open channel to the newest scientific research and nutritional advice plays a critical role. The field of nutrition is continually evolving, and keeping abreast of the latest findings can help refine and affirm your diet choices. For instance, recent studies highlighting the benefits of intermittent fasting or the roles of microbiomes in digestion might offer you insights that tweak your eating habits for the better.

However, flooding yourself with too much information can lead down a path of confusion. Strike a balance by selecting a few credible sources that resonate with your values and needs. Blogs, podcasts, webinars, and newsletters from respected institutions or certified nutrition experts can be a great start. Dedicate time each week to read or listen to this curated content to transform learning into a habit, not a chore.

Staying informed also means being wary of the pervasive myths and misinformation about dieting that abound. Developing a critical mind when evaluating the validity and source of information can protect you from false promises and harmful practices. Learning to spot red flags, such as quick-fixes or drastic results from minimal effort, can save you from setbacks in your wellness journey.

Apart from external inspiration, self-reflection is a potent tool. Keeping a journal or blog about your weight loss journey allows you to track your progress, understand your patterns, and acknowledge your successes. This process of self-reflection can also uncover deeper motivations and perceived barriers that you might not have noticed initially.

Technology, when used wisely, augments your arsenal of inspiration and information. Various apps offer not only tracking capabilities for diet and exercise but also provide motivational reminders and educational content. More importantly, many of these apps build communities where users can share experiences and support each other, thereby weaving a social fabric that enriches the solo journey of weight loss.

Setting periodic goals and celebrating when they are achieved can provide continuous motivation. These milestones can be as simple as improving your water intake, increasing your weekly walking distance, or mastering a new cooking technique. Celebrating these victories, small or large, reinforces positive behavior and helps in building a sustainable routine.

Preparation for inevitable setbacks by arming yourself with coping strategies is another facet of staying informed. Understanding that every journey has its ups and downs will prepare you emotionally, allowing you to navigate this with resilience rather than despair.

Finally, sharing your journey can not only inspire others but also reinforce your commitment. Whether through social media, a blog, or casual conversations, articulating your journey helps you internalize your achievements and challenges, embedding your commitment deeper into your identity.

In conclusion, keeping your mental and emotional game strong is fundamental to sustaining your weight loss efforts. By staying informed and inspired, you continually nourish the mindset necessary for long-term success. It's about building and maintaining a lifestyle that resonates not just with your body, but also with your heart and mind. Keep learning, remain inspired, and let every new piece of knowledge and every shared story be a stepping stone towards a healthier you.

11.3 CELEBRATING YOUR ACHIEVEMENTS AND SETTING NEW GOALS

In the journey of weight loss and healthier living, your victories—both large and small—are not just milestones, but powerful catalysts that propel you further along the path to wellness. Celebrating these achievements is not merely a suggestion; it's an essential strategy to cementing new habits and setting new, more ambitious goals. This process of acknowledgment and renewal reinforces your commitment and keeps the cycle of positive change revolving.

Imagine Jessica, who reached her initial weight loss goal of twenty pounds. She took a moment to reflect and celebrate this significant achievement, not by indulging in old eating habits but by treating herself to a new workout outfit, symbolizing her ongoing commitment to health. Jessica's celebration is a perfect blend of acknowledgment and motivation, encapsulating the balance between enjoying the present moment and looking forward to new challenges.

Acknowledging your accomplishments should cater to your personal tastes and respect your journey. For some, it might be a quiet evening with a book, a day at the spa, or purchasing a new kitchen gadget to support your culinary adventures with healthier foods. The key is to choose rewards that reaffirm your commitment to a healthy lifestyle rather than contradict it.

For an ongoing motivation, turn your achievements into stories to share. Telling your success stories to friends, family, or a supportive online community not only increases your sense of accountability but also inspires others. Moreover, vocalizing your successes can reinforce your identity as someone who values health and perseverance, integrating these traits more deeply into your self-conception.

However, the journey doesn't end with one goal met or one story told. It's equally important to set new, realistic objectives. As you evolve, so too should your goals. This could mean shifting focus towards gaining strength, improving endurance, or even learning more about nutritional science. Perhaps your next objective could be a physical challenge like a marathon, or maybe, it's learning and mastering the art of healthy Mediterranean cooking. The point is to keep evolving, pushing your boundaries just enough to remain challenged but not overwhelmed.

Setting new goals involves careful planning. Evaluate what worked in the prior phase: What habits did you find beneficial? Which strategies were less helpful? Applying these insights will help streamline your process as you move forward. Setting SMART goals—specific, measurable, attainable, relevant, and time-bound—can considerably enhance your ability to achieve them. These criteria ensure your objectives are clear and actionable, cultivating a path forward that is both structured and adaptable.

Balanced goal setting emphasizes both long-term ambitions and short-term objectives. The long-term goals provide a big picture to strive for, while the short-term goals serve as stepping stones that make the journey attainable and measurable. This dual-focus approach ensures you can celebrate small victories regularly, sustaining your motivation.

Reflecting on your journey periodically to reassess your goals is crucial. Life changes, and what may have been a relevant goal six months ago might not align with your current circumstances or understanding. Regular reflection, therefore, allows you to pivot and adapt, ensuring that your goals remain both challenging and achievable.

Accountability plays a significant role in sticking to your goals. Engaging with a buddy, hiring a coach, or being part of a community can provide the external motivation needed to stay on track. They can offer encouragement, share their insights, and help you navigate through rough patches. Just as importantly, they can celebrate with you, reinforcing the joy and satisfaction of achieving each goal.

In times of stagnation or struggle, it's essential to remember that progress in weight loss and health is not always linear. There will be periods of rapid progress and times when things slow down. During these slower times, maintaining focus on your overarching objectives, adjusting your strategies, and being patient are vital. Moreover, redefine your understanding of achievement; sometimes, maintaining progress, not just advancing, is a success in itself.

Finally, integrating these objectives into your day-to-day life must be done with care. This integration ensures that your goals don't remain abstract or distant but are living parts of your daily existence. Incorporate specific actions into your routine, make constant adjustments as required, and always align these actions with the broader context of your life.

Remember, every step you take toward celebrating your achievements and setting new goals is a step toward a healthier, more fulfilled you. It's not just about the weight you lose or the fitness levels you gain; it's about building a sustainable lifestyle that continuously enriches your life, reflecting ever-higher aspirations for health and happiness. Your journey is uniquely yours, and every success along the way deserves recognition and renewal.

THANK YOU FOR YOUR PURCHASE!

Dear Reader,

I am thrilled that you have chosen to explore my book, and I sincerely hope it brings you as much joy as I experienced during its creation. Your support is invaluable to me!

If you have a moment, I would deeply appreciate your leaving a review. Sharing your thoughts helps me grow as a writer and guides others in their choice of books.

As a special thank you, please scan the QR code below to receive exclusive bonus content I've prepared just for my readers.

Warmest thanks once again for your wonderful support.

Best wishes,

Ivy Villasenor

Made in the USA
Monee, IL
12 May 2025

17341676R00063